UNMET NEED

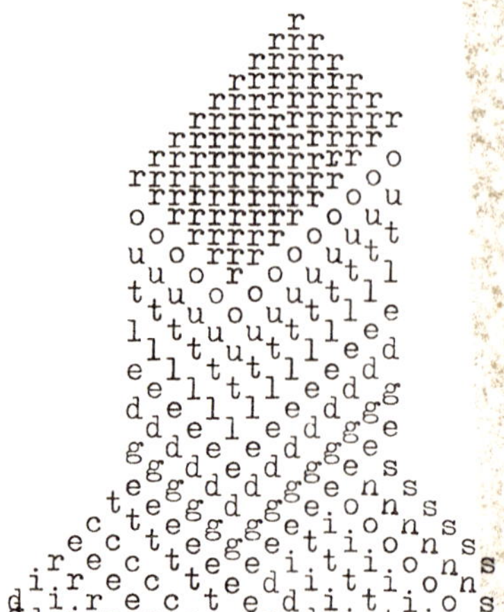

UNMET NEED
The Case of the Neighbourhood Law Centre

ANTHEA BYLES and PAULINE MORRIS

ROUTLEDGE DIRECT EDITIONS

ROUTLEDGE & KEGAN PAUL
London, Henley and Boston

First published in 1977
by Routledge & Kegan Paul Ltd
39 Store Street,
London WC1E 7DD,
Broadway House,
Newtown Road,
Henley-on-Thames,
Oxon RG9 1EN and
9 Park Street,
Boston, Mass. 02108, USA
Printed and bound in Great Britain by
Thomson Litho Ltd
East Kilbride, Scotland

British Library Cataloguing in Publication Data

Byles, Anthea
Unmet need.
1. North Kensington Neighbourhood Law Centre -
History
I. Title II. Morris, Pauline
362.5'8 HV685.G7 77-30042

ISBN 0-7100-8649-0

CONTENTS

TABLES

PREFACE

This study formed part of the work of the Legal Advice Research Unit and when the Unit was first set up, it was hoped that a number of alternative strategies for the delivery of legal services would be developed within its first year of operation, thereby providing an opportunity for monitoring and evaluating differently structured organizations with differing ideologies. In the event, despite much discussion amongst interested parties, these plans did not materialize, and for much of the life-span of the Unit, North Kensington remained the only law centre in existence. As a result, the research effort was of necessity largely directed into other channels, although an attempt was made to evaluate some of the newer law centres as they subsequently became established in the London area. Later, approaches were made to the newer centres with a view to undertaking research, but unfortunately these were unsuccessful, the staff being wary of the impact that such research might have on their work at such an early stage of development. Furthermore, at one centre some of the community representatives on the Management Committee felt that local residents would not like being 'researched', and they feared that to do so would cause loss of confidence in the centre.

Initial studies undertaken by the Unit during its first year of operation had led to the setting up of a new type of centre - the Newham Rights Centre - but once again the delay between the recommendation and the actual starting date meant that monitoring and evaluation could not take place within the life-time of the Unit.

We think it important that readers of the present volume should be aware of this background, because what had been intended as an overall study of law centres, or branches of law offices in poor areas of the city has, in practice, had to take the form of a case-study of one pioneer law centre (the field work for which was carried out during 1973). To place such a centre in 'floodlights' in many respects gives a false picture: in the process of intensive evaluation certain aspects of the work may have been given undue emphasis; had more comparative data been available these issues might well have assumed less significance. Almost by definition, being first in the field means that there will be mistakes and failures, and if we seem to have dwelled on these unduly it is in the hope that something useful can be learned by those who come after. For however critical one may be of North Kensington, for two-and-a-half years it remained the only neighbourhood law centre of its kind providing a full-time, free, legal service, and more recently established centres owe a great debt to the work done by this small group of pioneers.

ANTHEA BYLES, London, September 1976
PAULINE MORRIS, Vancouver, September 1976

ACKNOWLEDGMENTS

This study was one of a series funded by the Nuffield Foundation and forms part of the work of the Legal Advice Research Unit. We are grateful to the Foundation, and in particular to Dr Ken Blyth, former Assistant Director, and to Miss Pat Thomas who succeeded him. We also appreciate the support given by the Advisory Committee, whose comments on our earlier draft were most helpful.

We are grateful to the Management Committee of the Centre for allowing us access, and to the staff who tolerated a researcher in their midst during the year of the study. We appreciate their co-operation and forbearance during that time.

We would also like to thank all those individuals and groups in the neighbourhood who contributed to the research; the willingness of clients to be interviewed during the course of the field work was particularly helpful, as was the assistance given by the staff and volunteers of the Centre, members and ex-members of the Management Committee, and representatives of other local groups and organizations.

The interviewing of clients and other local residents, often involving long and awkward hours, was undertaken by an industrious band of interviewers; our thanks are due to Carel Peake, Jon Clare, Margaret Freeman and Frank Burton.

Valuable assistance in coding the interview material was received from Leslie Robinson and Mike Green whom we thank for their efforts.

Finally, we extend our gratitude to Isobel Leung who typed all material relating to the project and who patiently re-typed amended sections of the final draft.

Chapter 1

GENERAL BACKGROUND

The North Kensington Neighbourhood Law Centre, the first law centre in England, opened on 17 July 1970. Having been established at a time when there was growing concern about what was referred to, amongst legal and affiliated circles, as the 'unmet need for legal services', it has now (1974) completed its fourth year of work. Before considering the development of this particular centre, it is relevant to look briefly at the background surrounding the provision of legal services, against which North Kensington, and more recently, other law centres were set up. (1)

Legislation to allow poor people to have access to legal services has existed for several centuries. (2) However, a convenient point to take up the thread is in 1944, with the appointment of a committee of both lawyers and laymen, under the chairmanship of Lord Rushcliffe, to consider all aspects of legal aid and advice. (3)

Prior to the Second World War, the Poor Person's Rules, administered by the Law Society, allowed private practitioners to give their services without charge, but the pressures and disruptive effects of the war period, together with changes in the divorce law in 1937, brought increased demands which the existing framework was inadequate to meet. Some of these demands, for example those relating to matrimonial matters, were to a limited extent met by the introduction of new provisions such as the Services Divorce Department, set up by the Law Society in 1942, to act for servicemen and their wives, but in many areas of law the gaps remained large.

The report of the Rushcliffe Committee recognized that although much valuable work was being undertaken by voluntary advice centres (4) 'the great increase in legislation and the growing complexity of modern life have created a situation in which increasing numbers of people must have recourse to professional legal assistance.' (5) In the case of civil proceedings they recommended a scheme whereby legal aid was to be made available to a wider income group than 'those normally classed as poor'. The cost was to be borne by the state, but a sliding scale of contributions was to be used for those who could afford partial payment. The scheme was to be administered and controlled by the Law Society, rather than by any agency of local or central government, thereby keeping it under the wing of the legal profession. (6) The actual decision-making was to be undertaken by local committees, who in turn were appointed by area committees.

It was also proposed that the Law Society should be responsible for establishing a system whereby legal advice could be offered to low-income people with legal problems, it being hoped that the services of a lawyer at an early stage would obviate the need for litigation.

Different proposals were made for the administration of legal aid in criminal proceedings; here the decision to grant or withhold a legal aid order was to remain in the hands of the court, subject to a means test applied by the courts on the advice of the Home Office.

The recommendations of the Committee were broadly speaking adopted in the Legal Aid and Advice Act 1949, (7) thereby contributing to the wider social welfare legislation passed in the years immediately following the war.

However, by the time the Act was passed the country was facing severe financial problems; the costs of the welfare state were already exceeding the original estimates in every sphere, and as a consequence the new provisions for legal aid and advice were implemented only in stages.

However, financial strictures on the implementation of this post-war scheme were not the only barriers to its general acceptance. Despite a widespread campaign by members of the Council of the Law Society whereby they travelled the country in order to explain the nature of the scheme and to meet objections and allay fears, a considerable amount of criticism was expressed in the early years, emanating largely from the Bench. Judges found difficulty in accepting that legal aid should set people without means on an equality with paying clients and so have a right of access to the Courts which they had until then been denied; the concept of legal aid as a right, to be provided as an integral part of the welfare state was regarded as unacceptable. Indeed, from material collected during the research it would seem that this attitude has lingered on in some quarters to the present day. In interviews with clients of the Law Centre many complained of the negative views which they felt those working in the courts showed towards legally aided clients: one incident was recalled where a stipendiary magistrate had made quite clear his displeasure at 'yet another' litigant supported by public funds.

Although by 1965 many aspects of the Legal Aid and Advice Scheme had been implemented, largely those dealing with legal aid, the lack of an effective advice scheme may have robbed the scheme as a whole of much of its impact, since both were intended to form an integrated service. (8) In practice those sections of the Act dealing with legal advice were not introduced until ten years later.

Furthermore, by 1965 many of the original provisions of the Act had become outdated. Since its inception there had been problems in keeping the income limits at a realistic level, and difficulties and anomalies in administering the scheme were daily becoming more and more evident. In criminal proceedings magistrates were often unwilling to grant legal aid, particularly if the accused pleaded guilty; and many lawyers did not consider that they were properly remunerated and in consequence were reluctant to take on legally aided cases (even today they are paid only 90 per cent of their taxed costs in Supreme Court litigation).

In the civil scheme the control exercised by the legal profession through area and certifying committees ensured a concern for the protection of public funds which arguably was excessive. The Act required that legal aid be granted where the certifying committee considered that it was reasonable to take proceedings - a stipulation which has been interpreted as the applicant having a 'prima facie' case, and in addition 'where it would not be unreasonable in all the circumstances' to do so. This latter requirement has come to be interpreted as 'the test of the paying client': if such a client went to a private solicitor would he be advised to take proceedings? Many argue that, with certain exceptions, the result of these tests as applied by certifying committees, has been to elevate the financial aspects of legal disputes over those of justice.

A further criticism of the civil scheme concerned its limited scope inasmuch as defamation and proceedings before coroner's courts were excluded, but the most glaring omission was the fact that legal aid was not available for tribunal representation, an issue which affected large numbers of low-income people. In practice the scheme was used primarily for matrimonial cases - over 80 per cent of the certificates granted were in respect of divorces.

Finally it should be borne in mind when considering the civil scheme that lawyers themselves were generally speaking ill-equipped to deal with the problems of the poor by virtue of their training and their experience, which was largely limited to middle-class private practice. As a result there was little attempt made by the profession to seek out work of such a very different nature.

By the mid-1960s the limitations of the 1949 Act, to some extent a function of the failure to implement it as originally intended, were well recognised. In America at this time an increasing number of Federally funded neighbourhood law offices were being set up as part of the anti-poverty programme, with the aim of extending legal services to people in deprived urban areas. In this country, the Law Society, in a memorandum dated February 1968 (9) denounced such a concept on four grounds: they maintained that it would be socially divisive to have a separate legal aid system for the poor; that it would be wrong to have services under the ordinary legal aid scheme subject to contribution whilst the services available at local law centres would be free; that practitioners in such centres were likely to be either young and inexperienced or old and incompetent; and finally that the proposed new service would be prohibitively expensive and would require a new organization to run it. The Law Society's own proposals at this time centred on reviving and expanding the legal advice scheme, together with a plan whereby the Society would itself employ solicitors to act as liaison officers, in order to provide a link between lawyers in private practice and social welfare agencies operating in the local community. (10)

The debate was soon taken up on the political front when groups of lawyers representing both the main political parties made known their views on the matter and presented proposals for change in documents published in December 1968. In 'Rough Justice', a pamphlet issued by the Conservative Political Centre, it was recommended that, with the help of government subsidies, practising lawyers be encouraged to open branch offices in the poorest areas of cities. An alternative solution offered by the Society of Labour Lawyers in 'Justice for All' recommended the establishment of local legal centres on the model of the neighbourhood law firms in the USA. They argued that the absence of solicitors in the poorest areas could only be met by state-salaried lawyers operating without charge in places where they were most needed.

By July 1969 the Law Society, faced with mounting criticism of existing legal aid provisions from lawyers themselves, reversed its views with regard to neighbourhood law offices. A second memorandum was published in which it sought power itself 'to set up local legal centres', a proposal which was later to provide the basis for Part II of the Legal Advice and Assistance Act 1972. The need for a revision of the existing scheme was reiterated in the Law Society's twentieth annual report to the Lord Chancellor published in July 1971, (11) though the main emphasis in that document remained firmly on the need for developing an advisory service.

> Looking back it is apparent that the economic problems which attended the [Legal Aid] Scheme, preventing a full implementation of the 1949 Act, have resulted in some distortion in the development of the Scheme which ought now to be corrected. The complete absence of an advisory service during the major part of the first decade and the substitution of the existing advice scheme for the far wider provisions of Section 7 of the Legal Aid and Advice Act 1949, again for economic reasons, have resulted in laying the main emphasis upon the support of litigation. From the social point of view, this is unfortunate and it is important that the balance should be corrected by placing an equal emphasis upon the advisory services which a prudent citizen, with the means to do so, invokes to avoid finding himself in situations in which he may be faced with litigation. Moreover, the development of legal aid has inevitably been conditioned by the pattern of legal services which prevailed at the time the Scheme came into being. Since then, the need for advice and assistance has greatly increased and in many respects the nature of the help required has changed in character. The absence of an effective advisory service has resulted in the Scheme failing to keep pace with the social changes which have occurred through the Development of the Welfare State and other factors. (12)

Meanwhile, in the absence of any move by the government to provide funds to implement the proposals of either political party, further discussions amongst Labour Lawyers led certain of them to set about seeking financial support for establishing one or more law centres on an experimental basis. After prolonged negotiations with charitable trusts, the first of such centres opened its doors - in North Kensington.

Chapter 2

SETTING UP THE NORTH KENSINGTON NEIGHBOURHOOD LAW CENTRE

Today if you walk into the North Kensington Neighbourhood Law Centre it is a hive of activity combined with a slight air of confusion: volunteers being briefed on their next assignment; solicitors dropping in and out; visitors trying to find out how a place like this runs; the receptionist dealing with new enquiries and with clients who have come to keep appointments, as well as answering a constantly ringing telephone. From the outside, although the name is proclaimed in bold coloured lettering on a plate glass window, the Law Centre is unobtrusive; set up in a converted butcher's shop it blends completely with its surroundings in a busy market street, so well in fact that even members of staff have sometimes been known to walk past absent-mindedly!

But what lies behind the activity - what is it trying to achieve, what did it set out to achieve? Why was it set up in North Kensington? Who was involved in setting it up? In short, how did it all begin and why?

Why North Kensington? Traditionally North Kensington is a working-class area. In the nineteenth century pig-keepers settled in Notting Dale, the south-west corner of North Kensington, finding it more secluded than their previous homes near Marble Arch. In the same locality small brick-making businesses were established, and part of the area became known as the Potteries. This particular spot which was badly drained and unhealthy, was hit badly by a cholera epidemic in 1849 and was described by Dickens as being 'a plague-spot, scarcely equalled for its insalubrity by any other in London.... Nearly all the inhabitants look unhealthy.' (1) It was also an area well known for its criminality. Urban development coincided with the Great Exhibition and the building of the Metropolitan Railway in the mid-nineteenth century, when it became a matter of urgency to house the navvies employed on such work. The bad conditions in the area have been the cause of much comment over many years; in 1889 Booth cited a report by the local medical officer of health which described it as being 'as God forsaken as anything in London'. (2) Over sixty years later, Martin Adeney, (3) was to describe North Kensington in the following way:

> it has been a case history in the primers of poverty for the past century. It has been known as a place of demoralising over-

crowding in bad housing dominated by some ruthless landlordism and also as a last refuge for the low income family with children, who finds difficulty in getting accommodation of any sort in central London.

Since the mid-nineteenth century the area has remained densely populated: it forms part of the Royal Borough of Kensington and Chelsea which, although it is the smallest borough in London, has the highest density of persons per acre (60.2). (4) Nearly a third of the borough's population lives in North Kensington yet it contains almost half the children aged up to 15 for the whole of the borough. (5) It has always been in the position of 'poor relation' within the second richest London borough: in South Kensington there are nine children for every one tenth of an acre of open space, in North Kensington the same area accommodates eighty-nine children. (6)

Furthermore North Kensington has traditionally been an area where immigrants to Britain have settled, often from Ireland, from Africa, from the West Indies (particularly in the 1950s) and more recently from Mediterranean countries. Many work in the service sector of the employment market, responding to the chronic need for such workers in central London:

> If London is to have more hotels and restaurants, more places of entertainment, and a greater range of personal services of all kinds, with more shops, we shall have an increasing demand for the workers who now receive the lowest 25 per cent of personal incomes in the Metropolitan area.... Without them the Metropolis cannot function. They cannot commute from a distance: their incomes will not allow it, and the transport system cannot take them.... We cannot leave them where they are: their dwellings are often obsolete and insanitary. (7)

In 1958 the so-called 'race riots' hit the national headlines and the attendant publicity was responsible for creating a notorious image for Notting Hill. (8) These events centred on incidents occurring in the last week of August and the first week of September 1958:

> 'On the night of Saturday-Sunday, 23-24 August, three incidents occurred to start the main disturbances around Notting Dale. In the first a coloured man was attacked at a public house in Notting Hill by some white men, who struck him with 'dustbin lids and broken milk bottles'.... At one o'clock that morning milk bottles were thrown at the windows of two houses occupied by coloured people in Bramley Road, in the centre of Notting Dale. Between three and five the same morning, in various parts of Notting Hill, six West Indians were attacked and badly injured by teddy boys wielding iron bars. Nine youths were arrested.... It was they who were later sentenced to terms of imprisonment of four years each....
>
> On Sunday night, 31 August, a crowd of 200 whites gathered in Bramley Road and started to shout at coloured people. The crowd later grew to about 700; fifteen whites and four coloured men were arrested, but not before two police cars had been damaged.
>
> The national papers of Monday, 1 September, splashed the story of the night's incidents, many of the reports were distorted and misleading. Monday night began with a number of incidents in the Notting Hill area, one of which was the first and only effective

fascist meeting...although about 700 people were involved. Some coloured people retaliated by throwing bottles from the upper storeys of houses but in general they appeared to be frightened and to be avoiding notice. Several people were injured, with windows of five houses smashed and a door broken down.' (9)

These events attracted a large number of professional workers and academics to the area in order to study the problems, and many who live there now consider North Kensington to be over-researched; as one resident put it: 'It's a glass-cage for sociologists.'

The information summarised in Table 2.1 may help to give a picture of social conditions in North Kensington by comparison with the rest of the Borough. It is based upon statistical data obtained during the first year of the Unit's work, at which time only the 1966 census figures were available; these were supplemented by more up-to-date statistics supplied to the researcher by various social welfare agencies. (10) The use of social indicators involves many methodological problems reflecting as they do the absence of a firm theoretical background. (11) It is recognized that the inclusion of a particular factor may be justifiable in 'common-sense' terms, but its selection may well be a reflection of the researcher's own value-judgments; furthermore an indicator may be as much a reflection of local provision as of local need, and it is therefore essential that these findings be interpreted with great caution.

Travelling from the south to the north of the Borough the stark physical and social contrasts are very apparent; the wealthy residential and shopping areas of South Kensington and Chelsea are replaced by dilapidated housing and grim conditions in the North of the Borough. From the table it is clear that there is a heavy concentration of problems in North Kensington; out of the sixteen social indicators shown, North Kensington wards are placed on all but two factors (mobility and old age) and on nine of the factors the problem indicated exists in 3 out of 4 of the electoral wards.

Since 1958 there has been a considerable amount of voluntary group activity in North Kensington aimed at improving local conditions. In 1959 a Methodist Group Ministry was set up in Notting Hill using a grass roots approach to community work, and one of its ministers founded the Notting Hill Social Council in 1960. This provided a forum for both statutory and voluntary social workers and at the same time was responsible for developing a variety of projects intended to help specific groups in the community, such as the Blenheim Project for out-of-town 'drifters', and the Portobello Project for unattached youth.

In 1966 the Notting Hill Community Workshop was established, followed shortly afterwards by the Notting Hill People's Association. A year later, the Community Workshop initiated the Notting Hill Summer Project, an early attempt at action-research to be undertaken by a coalition of local groups, and organized by an independent committee comprising community workers and clergy active in the area. However, the coalition was short lived and strongly divisive splits and factions emerged between the various voluntary agencies. The resulting tensions, reflecting as they did the differing ideologies of the organizations concerned, led at the time to the setting up of the Notting Hill Housing Service (later known as the Housing Action

TABLE 2.1 Ward ranking in distribution of social indicators in Kensington and Chelsea

Note: Rankings 1-4 denote wards with highest concentrations of each indicator	Overcrowding	Shared/no facilities	Rent tribunal applications	Possession orders	Born overseas	Moved within last year	Classes IV, V	Free school meals	Debt	60, 65+	Under 5	Married women at work	Mentally ill	Subnormal	EPA index*	Nos appearing before Juvenile Bureau
N. KENSINGTON																
Golborne	1	1	1	1			1	3	1		1		1	2	1	1
St Charles	3	2					3		2		2	2	4	3		
Pembridge	4	4		3	4			1	3		4	1	2		2	2
Norland			4				2				3		3	1	4	3
S. KENSINGTON																
Holland																
Earls Court	2		2		1	1		4							3	
Queens Gate						4										
Redcliffe					2	2		2								
Brompton					3	3										
Hans Town				4						3						
CHELSEA																
North Stanley										4						4
South Stanley		3					4					4		4		
Church			3							1						
Cheyne				2					4			3				
Royal Hospital										2						

* This ranking refers to wards containing primary and infant schools scoring highest on the ILEA index of Educational Priority Areas.

Centre), and many of these conflicts are still evident among some of the groups working in North Kensington today. (12)

In the first chapter we briefly traced the background which led the Society of Labour Lawyers to recommend the introduction of neighbourhood law firms. In August 1968, prior to this recommendation, a conference of Labour Lawyers had been held in Oxford, attended by, amongst others, those who were later to form the nucleus of founder members of the North Kensington Neighbourhood Law Centre, including an academic lawyer who had been prominent in the preparation of 'Justice for All' and who had recently returned from North America with first-hand knowledge of American Neighbourhood Law Firms.

The solicitor who was later to become the senior member of the Centre had for some time prior to this meeting been actively involved in organizing two evening advice sessions in North Kensington, first for the Community Workshop and later for the People's Association, and he was becoming increasingly frustrated by the limitations imposed on a service which could offer only advice. He therefore viewed with enthusiasm the possibility of setting up a centre which would provide a complete solicitor's service to all those living in the neighbourhood.

Following the Oxford conference several who had attended, including the solicitor mentioned above and a number of senior members of the profession, formed a working party with a view to developing outline proposals for a neighbourhood law centre. They were joined in this by community workers already involved in the area and the need for a centre was expressed in the following terms:

> For some time past many social agencies and organisations operating in North Kensington have been concerned at the inadequacy of the legal services which are readily available to the poor. It is inevitable that in an area of acute housing stress, with a large immigrant population, many people are in need of specialist legal advice, often urgent, and often requiring an appearance at court or tribunals. (13)

The proposal went on to outline the existing provision of legal services in the area; only one solicitor's office offered services to poor people, either under legal aid or at a nominal fee. This firm had been set up by a woman solicitor with the deliberate aim of providing a legal/social service rather than operating as a profit-making enterprise. In addition a limited number of people were being referred to private solicitors by the CAB. However, in order to comply with what were believed to be the requirements of the Law Society, the CAB could only show clients a list of available solicitors; they were prohibited from making specific recommendations. Furthermore the experience of local CAB workers suggested that people referred in this way did not always reach a solicitor, or if they did, they might find themselves faced with high fees as a result. Two voluntary organizations in the area offered legal advice once a week, as did both the Labour and Conservative Parties.

The group proposed that the functions of the neighbourhood law centre should be as follows:

> The service provided at such a centre would be analogous to that provided by the traditional family doctor. Thus the lawyers by working there would become accepted as part of the community, which would help to break down the anxiety prevalent among poor

people and likely, as has been shown, to inhibit them from obtaining help even though they have a good case. In the Law Centre, an atmosphere could be created between client and lawyer in which the taking of legal advice becomes for poor people less of a hazardous adventure. We would hope to bring about some degree of informality consistent with efficiency, and we envisage some visits being arranged where the social or legal circumstances require them. (14)

The proposals having been mapped out, the problems of funding the Centre and negotiating its terms of reference with the Law Society now had to be attempted. The advantages of independent funding were agreed by all those involved at the planning stage; in any case it was thought that government money was unlikely to be forthcoming, unwillingness to provide further funds having been a major factor in preventing the extension of legal aid provisions under the 1949 Act. The working party considered that there would be serious disadvantages to local authority funding since, over such major issues as housing, there would inevitably be a conflict of interest, with the local authority being the 'other party'. (15)

It was therefore decided to seek support from charitable institutions and a number of grant-giving bodies were approached. The task of 'selling' was not an easy one, but the organizers were helped by the presence of a number of 'establishment' figures on the working party.

Eventually grants totalling £9,000 were received from two foundations, (16) to last over a period of three years, and this enabled the Centre to open. In the first year £4,000 of this sum was available and there was a projected income of £4,000 from legal aid. (17) The decision to open was further made possible by the fact that only £470 was charged annually by the local authority to cover rent and rates.

With the support of the local Law Society (the West London Law Society) waivers were applied for from the parent body in order to allow the Centre to advertise and to handle free of charge such cases as did not fall within the terms of reference of the Legal Aid Scheme, for example welfare problems and tribunal work. As was mentioned earlier, in a memorandum published in July 1969, the Law Society had itself sought powers 'to set up permanent local centres... adapted to the general needs of the district including, if necessary, representation in magistrates courts and county courts and the conduct of litigation so far as this cannot be absorbed by solicitors' firms'; (18) it was thus favourably disposed to an experimental scheme being set up in North Kensington, and the necessary waivers were granted in October 1969.

In order to be eligible for charitable funding and to qualify for tax exemptions, it was necessary for the Centre to become a registered charity. This entailed submitting its constitution to the Charity Commissioners for approval, one concern of that body being to ensure that the service offered is directed to 'poor people' and that 'political' activity is not involved. (19) The constitution satisfied the commissioners and charitable status was accordingly granted in August 1970.

These major administrative difficulties having been surmounted, there remained the practical problem of premises. A short-life property was leased from the local authority at a peppercorn rent (£4 per week); it was guaranteed for two years at least, and although at the time of writing four years have elapsed there is still no date fixed for vacating it. To make the building suitable for use as a law centre everyone concerned rallied round. (20) In the few weeks preceding 17 July 1970, the official opening date, the final touches were being made to the shop, and during this period the first member of staff, who later became the senior solicitor, ran the Centre from his home, with the help of a secretary, and for part of the time with an articled clerk.

During its third and fourth years additional funding was made available by the Nuffield Foundation. At the same time a request was made by the Foundation that a programme of research and evaluation be carried out by the Legal Advice Research Unit. The original plan included the evaluation of a number of alternative methods of delivering legal services, but this proved impracticable, and comparative data are not available. This clearly limits the value of the present study; nevertheless much of the controversy that originally surrounded the establishment of law centres still persists and the present case-history of one law centre may help to throw into relief some of the wider problems currently associated with schemes aiming to offer an alternative system for the delivery of legal services.

RESEARCH (21)

In planning the research we drew heavily on North American experience. (22) The evaluation was designed to operate at two levels:

(a) to assess the impact of the centre, not only upon clients, but upon the community in general and upon other agencies providing services;

(b) to assess the effectiveness of the centre in achieving predicted outcomes or intended goals.

Prior to starting such in-depth research, the Legal Advice Research Unit had, as part of its wider study of unmet need, undertaken a more general study of the London Borough of Kensington and Chelsea in which the Law Centre was situated. In addition to demographic, social and economic data, details of existing legal facilities and social welfare provisions were obtained and some assessment of inter-agency relationships and attitudes was made. Finally, a pilot study was carried out amongst members of the public living in certain areas of the borough in order to determine - amongst other things - the kinds of legal and/or socio-legal problems which they faced, their views concerning services currently available to meet their needs, and their attitudes to the law and to the legal system. (23)

In undertaking the study of the Law Centre an attempt was made to combine both quantitative and qualitative approaches and since it was recognized that the delivery of a particular service to a community requires a continuous process of 'accommodation' between the agency and that community, it was decided that one researcher should spend a full year at the Centre assisted, as necessary, by interviewers; in this way it was hoped to avoid a too static approach.

Details of the research method, together with a discussion of the problems arising are given in Appendix A. The following brief outline gives an indication of the nature of the work undertaken:

(i) a study of record cards and reception day-book to determine the range and type of problems brought to the Centre;

(ii) interviews with 150 clients to study factors precipitating their approach to the Centre, any contact with other agencies in the area, the specific expectations they brought to the Centre, their views of the service offered, their attitudes to the law and legal services generally;

(iii) interviews with 5 full-time legal staff (including one past member), 12 evening volunteers and 13 management committee members (past and present), to examine the policies and goals of the Centre as perceived at different levels;

(iv) attendance at all committee and staff meetings and a content analysis of all committee minutes to study the internal organization of the agency, covering topics such as finance, staffing, administration, management, etc.;

(v) interviews with 12 (24) members of staff of other agencies in the area concentrating on the relationship of the Centre with the wider community and other resources within it, how these other agencies viewed its work, how much use they made of it and the Centre of them;

(vi) observation of the Centre's relationship with the newly emerging law centres and any influence this had on the direction of its work, particularly at the community level e.g. test cases, law reform, attempts to influence legislation or local government policy, etc.;

(vii) interviews with 100 local residents who had not used the Centre in order to discuss whether they knew of its availability and whether they had similar needs or problems which might have been referred to the agency, and if so, how had they dealt with these.

Considerable emphasis was placed upon item (ii), follow-up interviews with clients, since we were aware that many American researchers concerned with evaluating the OEO Legal Services Program had experienced great difficulty in obtaining access to clients. (25) Forewarned by this experience we went to considerable lengths to obtain permission to carry out intensive interviews with clients of the Centre with a view to evaluating the help and advice given in terms of its relevance to the client. (26)

The fieldwork took place two-and-a-half years after the Centre opened its doors to the public, and the results of the survey are reported in the following chapters.

THE DEVELOPMENT OF THE CENTRE

In describing the growth and development of the Centre, some of the problems will be highlighted, and the ways in which these have been handled at various stages in its history will be discussed. Much of the material used in this chapter is based upon extensive reference to the Centre's records, and to reports of meetings, many of them dating back to the time it was set up. In addition, a considerable amount of information was obtained in interviews with founder members, and with staff and committee members both past and present. These interviews produced much subjective material and in the following sections several issues are raised which were central to discussions at committee meetings and which at times caused considerable friction between certain members of the committee and some members of staff. However, it is by no means intended to convey that there was a constant or an accumulating conflict; at a personal level relationships remained for the most part very amicable.

At the time of opening, the aims of the Centre were very specific. It was to provide a solicitor's service to the people of a deprived area. The general enthusiasm which supported this concept had not allowed for a great deal of discussion about the way the Centre was to be run, nor had a great deal of consideration been given to broader issues such as the Centre's relationship with the community. It was originally hoped that a staff of three full-time solicitors and one community worker could be appointed, but the available funds would only support one full-time solicitor, a secretary/receptionist and an articled clerk. Forty members of the local Law Society offered their services on a voluntary basis in the evenings, but although the senior solicitor clearly envisaged their involvement being exclusively in the capacity of evening clerks, little detailed thought had been given to the precise ways in which such help might be organized.

This lack of consideration concerning the structural organization and administration of the Centre applied to all aspects of its work; it was understood that the senior solicitor was appointed to run the Centre on a day-to-day basis, but overall responsibility for policy decisions, as well as for funding, lay with the Management Committee. The constitution contained a clause calling for the setting up of an Advisory Council 'to consider the work of the Centre in the context of its relationship with the community in the Centre's area'.

In the early days discussions on such vital matters as staffing, internal administration, limitations of the caseload, referrals to other agencies and to private solicitors, dominated the Management Committee meetings. Those responsible for setting up the Law Centre were united in their belief that there was a very real need for such a centre, but bearing in mind their differing backgrounds and professional skills it was perhaps inevitable that they should have had differing expectations concerning its goals, and the ways in which these might be achieved. With the benefit of hindsight it is easy to say that many of the Centre's subsequent problems need never have arisen had there been more effective planning in the early days. However, in some measure this was precluded by the experimental nature of the Centre, and some might argue that the open nature of the decision-making process allowed it to develop in a more truly innovative and creative way than might have been possible had there been a greater degree of consensus, or a more clearly defined and hierarchical structure. We now turn to consider the different components of the organisation of the Centre in more detail.

THE MANAGEMENT COMMITTEE

This committee had ultimate responsibility for the work of the Centre and for the financial arrangements. It was a self-elected (1) body whose membership in the early days coincided to a large extent with the original working party. The constitution called for a membership of not less than 5 and not more than 15, including 6 members of the original working party and one representative each from the local Law Society, the local CAB and the Notting Hill Social Council, and three representatives from the Advisory Council. (2)

The composition of the committee has remained relatively static; such changes as have taken place have for the most part been members of the staff, and there have been four co-options to replace less active members (or members who have resigned).

Membership could be broadly divided into three groups, though often with overlapping professional backgrounds: founder members, members of the legal profession and representatives of local organizations and agencies. The second group included the legal staff of the Centre, as well as a representative from the local Law Society.

From the beginning there were differences of opinion amongst members as to the precise areas of competence with which the committee should concern itself. Whilst there was fairly general agreement that such matters as finance, staffing, the size of the catchment area and the nature of work to be undertaken were all legitimate topics for the Management Committee to consider and decide upon, there appeared to be less consensus on some other matters, notably the extent to which they should be involved in decisions regarding the internal administration of the Centre. As time elapsed and the financial problems facing the Centre grew more acute, some committee members expressed dismay that meetings were dominated by this particular topic, or with the problem of relations between the Centre and solicitors in private practice, to the neglect of wider, and seemingly more policy-oriented questions such as what the centre could or should be doing. In addition there were complaints from non-staff members of the committee that they were not kept properly informed about the Centre's activities.

The Management Committee was also critical of staff unwillingness to place clear-cut proposals before them for consideration; one member referred to the presentation of 'half-baked' ideas and to the absence of full information upon which to base decisions. Examples given included such matters as staff salaries, the need for additional staff (and of what kind) and items relating to costs and expenditure. (3)

The complaint that staff views were not clearly presented to them must be seen in the wider context of relationships between the committee and the staff. Attempts by the latter to avoid a hierarchical system of administration, and to create a democratic forum for decision-making, made it difficult (and often impossible) for a consensus view to be presented to the committee. Several of its members would have preferred that a 'general' staff view be presented by the senior solicitor, and in fact saw this as an essential part of his duties. However, neither he, nor most other members of staff, shared such a view: although nominally head of the Centre he did not see it as his function to co-ordinate staff opinions in this way, being more concerned to ensure that they all attended committee meetings and presented their own individual viewpoints. Thus whilst many committee members would have liked to benefit from the experience of staff who were involved in the day-to-day running of the Centre, they were presented with conflicting, and often confused, ideas from which they were expected to make a choice.

The fact that all the staff were encouraged to attend Management Committee meetings and to express their own viewpoint also created other difficulties, in particular for the non-legal members. They found themselves unable to communicate with committee members and some complained that the atmosphere was so formal that they were inhibited from making any contribution at all to the discussion. There was a suggestion that the lawyers seemed always to dominate the proceedings, a view also shared by some lay members of the committee itself, who expressed the view that they felt at a disadvantage when professional matters were being discussed. Whilst the lawyers denied that this occurred, the general opinion being that meetings were much less formal since the resignation of the first chairman who was said to have dominated proceedings, observation by the research worker indicated that it was indeed the general tendency at most committee meetings.

In the early days of the Centre there was a move by the first chairman of the Management Committee to separate lay and legal members and to create an 'inner sanctum' of legal members. This move was strongly resisted by lay members who felt that it would be undesirable for the lawyers to discuss policy in isolation, that is without the benefit of views purporting to represent the wider community.

There were other areas of staff/Management Committee conflicts: staff were critical of committee members on the grounds that they were not sufficiently active in seeking funds for the Centre. One committee member who agreed with this view nevertheless pointed out that it was a situation inherent in all voluntary committees - they are made up of high status, busy people who have insufficient time to devote to voluntary work of this nature. As a result it is only in a crisis situation that they become really active.

Certain legal members of the committee were especially fearful about the 'political' activity of certain staff members, and this proved to be a recurrent topic at both staff and Management Committee meetings. This concern was felt very strongly by those committee members who thought that the Centre's work should be exclusively directed towards the provision of a solicitor's service to local residents on a one-to-one basis. There was apprehension that they might affiliate themselves with certain outside activities and organizations as 'Law Centre staff' rather than as individuals, and by so doing it was feared that the staff would cause damage to the reputation of the Centre, and more particularly to the legal profession as a whole. (4) Examples of actions defined as 'political' included trade union membership, participation in demonstrations or strikes, and public involvement in controversy with the local council. It was not merely that such incidents themselves caused concern, but a sense of mistrust was engendered, with certain committee members feeling that a programme of political involvement was being planned about which they were being kept in ignorance.

When the Centre first opened, these (and other) conflicts were scarcely apparent, partly because of the general air of goodwill generated by a pioneering project, and partly because all those concerned were personally well known to each other, a situation which resulted in a good deal of informal as well as formal contact. However, as the size of the unit expanded and staff representation on the committee changed, there was less personal contact and some committee members admitted that they had been unable to visit the Centre as frequently as they ought, a situation they readily interpreted as a failure on their part. (5)

Two alternative suggestions were made with a view to resolving the conflicts: some members of staff and two committee members felt that the Management Committee had fulfilled its role by setting up the Centre and that it should be disbanded and replaced by an Advisory Council representing community interests. Others proposed that the Management Committee be expanded to include all members of the existing Advisory Council, not merely the three representatives demanded by the constitution. Neither of these alternatives was in fact adopted; however, the research and development officer appointed at the beginning of the research year was responsible for instituting a system of monthly reports to the Committee, with a view to obviating breakdowns in communication.

THE ADVISORY COUNCIL

When plans for establishing the Centre were first formulated, it was proposed that an Advisory Council should be set up consisting of local residents, clients, and representatives of local groups. The crucial role of the Advisory Council was to feed the Management Committee with ideas arising out of their personal knowledge and experience of the area, and to make suggestions concerning the direction of the work to be undertaken by the Centre. At the same time it was hoped that this would be a two-way process and that members of the Advisory Council would keep the community informed about the Centre's activities. The channel of communication was to be via the election of three representatives to the Management Committee.

In practice the first Advisory Council was slow to get off the ground and the first meeting did not take place until 20 months after the Centre opened. After three abortive and ill-attended meetings it ceased to function altogether. Those who attended were unsure of the purpose of the meetings and of the role of the Council generally. Reports of these meetings as submitted to the Management Committee indicate clearly that the role as initially envisaged was by no means understood by those who attended, and issues discussed were somewhat mundane: responsibility for the waiting room and its redecoration, the installation of a coffee machine, whether a room could be made available to the local community as a discussion centre (in which law centre clients could be involved), attendance of Advisory Council members at the Centre, and the design of notices explaining the Law Centre to clients.

After a lapse of seven months it was decided that an attempt should be made to reconvene the Council. This decision coincided with the appointment of a research and development officer who spent much of the first six months of his time considering the reasons for the demise of the original council and questioning those concerned about their expectations were it to be revived. It was recognized that if it were to be successful, Advisory Council members needed to feel a sense of involvement in the Centre's activities: complaints abounded concerning the peripheral nature of the earlier council and its lack of direction and clarity of purpose. To combat this, the research and development officer assumed responsibility for servicing the council and keeping members informed of the Centre's activities.

Whilst it was the original intention that local residents and clients (or ex-clients) of the Centre should be active on the council, in practice it consisted almost exclusively of representatives of local voluntary welfare agencies. By the time the research ended, it had just begun to suggest areas of community action in which the Law Centre might usefully intervene. (6)

STAFFING

Plans for staffing the Centre, apart from the allocation of solicitors, always presented difficulties, not least because the fluctuating financial situation made it difficult to employ enough staff. Initially, as has been mentioned, the staff comprised one solicitor, one articled clerk and one secretary. At that stage the nature of the enterprise was very experimental, but it soon became evident that the demand for help was enormous and the caseload rapidly overwhelmed the existing staff. (7) After approximately four months a second secretary was appointed and she recalled the situation at that time as being 'fairly chaotic'; reception was run by volunteers, there was no appointments system and there was a lack of continuity in relation to clients.

At various times in the Centre's history the idea of appointing a solicitor-advocate was mooted, it being suggested that such a person would save considerable sums in Counsel's fees. (8) At the same time it was thought that a solicitor-advocate would help with the existing caseload, rather than expand it, as would be the case if another solicitor were to be appointed. However, by the time approval for such an appointment was received from the Management Committee, one of the many financial crises had overtaken the Centre and no further appointments could be made. However, this also coincided with one of the full-time solicitors leaving the Centre and he then agreed to undertake part-time solicitor-advocate work for them on an experimental basis.

Early plans for the Centre specifically mentioned that the complement of legal staff would be strengthened by the appointment of a community worker. However this plan did not materialize: initially the pressure of individual casework was felt to make it necessary to concentrate on the appointment of legal staff (and secretaries to service them), and later, when applications were made to various charitable organizations for the funding of a community worker, these were unsuccessful. Had the Management Committee been unanimous in supporting such a move earlier on, it is possible that despite these difficulties an appointment would have been pushed through, but even when, at a later date, funds were forthcoming, and the proposal was put before the committee, some of the more senior legal members were wary of the implications of such an appointment, (9) and one member insisted that the position should be filled only if it could be done 'without detriment to the Centre's funds'. This ambivalence on the part of the committee coincided with a review of the Centre's administration and it was decided that the appointment of a full-time receptionist would make a more significant contribution to the work of the Centre.

Largely as a result of the failure to carry through the plans for appointing a community worker, an alternative proposal was put forward for the appointment of a research and development officer, and during much of the research period this matter was a cause of considerable controversy. It was intended that the post should be an experimental one, and although various areas of work were suggested in the original job description, the role of the person to be appointed was not clearly defined. It was agreed that a high degree of flexibility would enable the incumbent to develop in whatever ways suited his or her particular skills and interests, as well as seeming relevant to the perceived needs of the Centre. The appointment was made with some reservations and on the understanding that it would be critically reviewed after three months, and that during that period the work of the person appointed would be supervised by a sub-committee of the Management Committee. In the event this sub-committee did not meet during the three month period, but the Management Committee nevertheless laid some blame on the staff for not directing or supervising the research and development officer's activities adequately.

The lack of supervision highlighted the drawbacks to such an open-ended approach to the job. Without direction, a successful outcome depended upon the appointment of a person with strong and innovative views about relevant developments, as well as someone secure enough in his own professionalism to withstand domination by the lawyers. Unfortunately this proved not to be the case; the person appointed was a newcomer to the country, with no legal background and who, initially at least, interpreted his role as being largely that of a PR man 'showing the flag for the Centre' as he put it. Foremost among his duties he visualized reviving the Advisory Council meetings, thereby strengthening links with the community - at least at a formal level.

Second, such an open-ended appointment assumed a united view by other staff members of the perceived needs of the Centre and of the direction in which it was intended to develop, a situation which, as it was suggested earlier, simply did not exist. However if there was no consensus amongst the staff as to what his role should be, as time went by there was certainly agreement that his approach did not meet their varying expectations. It was rather vaguely supposed that he would undertake legal research, which would include the investigation of points of law and the collation of information from the Centre's several thousand cases, with a view to providing material for test cases and for the preparation of journal papers. Non-legal aspects of his research role were expected to include keeping abreast of general developments in the Borough, and investigating local issues which were known to be causing concern, such as property speculation, malpractices on the part of landlords and failure by the local authority to comply with regulations.

It seems likely that to some extent the confusion about his role stemmed from the earlier intention to appoint a community worker; some members of staff, as well as some of those on the Management Committee, undoubtedly hoped to emphasize the community aspect of the role (and in so far as the person appointed came from a background of such work this seemed a realistic expectation), whereas others would have preferred the emphasis to be on legal research linked specifically to the perceived needs of the local residents.

After a period of one year the appointment was terminated; by then, too, plans for a Housing Unit were under way and it was proposed that a research worker specializing in housing issues should be attached to it. If funds were available to support further help, then the original idea for the appointment of a community worker was to be revived, the person appointed being able to supplement the work of the Housing Unit.

From the initial small corps of staff, numbers increased and for most of the research period there was a total of twelve: 3 solicitors, 1 articled clerk, 1 full-time and 1 part-time receptionist, a research and development officer, a book-keeper, and 3 full-time and 1 part-time secretaries. As was pointed out earlier, although it was largely through the efforts of the senior solicitor that the Centre was set up, it was never his intention to assume a position of administrative leadership, and it was his hope that organizationally the Centre should remain acephalous. The careful selection of staff ensured that this ideology was generally shared, and so long as the size of the Unit remained small he was able to act almost exclusively as a legal case-worker and as adviser to other members of the team, so that few problems ensued. (10) However, as the work of the Centre expanded and the number of staff increased, his role changed imperceptibly, and of necessity he became increasingly involved in administrative duties, a situation he viewed with considerable ambivalence. At times his reluctance to be directive inhibited decision-making and made it difficult for other staff (particularly non-legal members) to have any clear idea of their role. Had there been agreement amongst the legal staff regarding the goals of the Centre, the absence of clear leadership might not have mattered; alternatively, had the conflicting goals been made more explicit, this might have led to a more obviously constructive outcome. But whilst there was some general agreement that the Centre should make a lawyer's service available to those who do not normally have such access, there was considerably less agreement as to what ends these services were intended to achieve, and hence there were differing perceptions about the means of achieving them. By glossing over the differences, at least at a formal level, a semblance of unity could be maintained and compromises reached.

Differences of opinion existed between those members of staff who wished to concentrate upon a casework function - providing an individualized service to those living in the area - and those who believed that the law should be used as a resource, a means of promoting social change. For the few who supported this view the eventual aim of the Centre could be seen as contributing to the creation of an 'a-legal' society, although it was recognized that in the short term the lawyers at the Centre would be engaged in a process of demystification and in helping residents 'fight the system'.

Within these two differing approaches there were, of course, much finer distinctions: for example the 'casework' approach blurred with a 'social work' approach, particularly when applied to civil rather than criminal proceedings. The potentially abrasive nature of the more 'political' approach (11) was modified by those who viewed access to the law as a means of achieving law reform, either by pointing up anomalies in existing legislation, or by undertaking test cases and class actions. The wealth of material available to the Centre concerning relatively uncharted and specialized issues of law was seen by some to provide the necessary background for such developments.

An alternative interpretation of the 'political' approach was presented by non-legal members of the Management Committee. They would have preferred to see the Centre more actively involved as a pressure group, supporting other organizations concerned with local issues such as housing and immigration.

The failure to formalize these issues and to work them through in terms of decision-making unfortunately prevented any clear-cut path of development for the Centre and at the same time allowed differences of opinion to develop both between staff and between staff and the Management Committee. (12)

VOLUNTARY HELP

In addition to the permanent, salaried, staff there were approximately seventeen legal volunteers, each working in the Centre one evening a week, or on Saturday mornings. They were predominantly solicitors engaged in private practice during the day-time, several from city firms specializing in commercial and company law and so having little experience of working with individual clients. Some volunteers were articled clerks for whom the work of the Centre provided a contrast from private practice; one described the weekly session at North Kensington as 'the high spot of the legal week'. (13)

The only form of training that legal volunteers received was to sit-in at a few interviews before undertaking any themselves; however, some were plunged in at the deep end, without even the benefit of this brief introduction. Whilst the majority felt that this kind of observation was the best method of training, some would have welcomed notes giving a résumé of those areas of law most frequently dealt with at the Centre. (14)

Most volunteers held quite realistic views concerning the nature of the work they were able to undertake in such a setting, seeing it in terms of doing some of the 'donkey work' for the full-time staff and allowing an evening service to be offered to clients. In view of the very heavy caseload carried by the Centre, it is perhaps surprising that little consideration appears to have been given to the desirability of expanding the use of legal volunteers. To recruit, train and supervise them would, of course, have taken up the time of the full-time lawyers, but it seems possible that they could have been trained to do some of the tasks which the staff of the Centre complained were neglected, such as community education or legal research.

Some volunteers complained that apart from their interviews with clients they felt isolated and were not made to feel part of the Centre by the full-time staff. However the suggestion that they might attend staff meetings received a mixed reception; some thought it would serve no useful purpose, whilst others saw such meetings as a potentially useful source of information, as well as providing an opportunity for involvement in policy decisions and as a social forum.

The majority of those working in private practice saw work in a neighbourhood law centre as providing a new and challenging type of work, but it was nevertheless not seen by the majority as a viable full-time alternative, mainly for financial reasons. The difference between this work and work in other settings, and to which attention was drawn most frequently in interviews, concerned the approach to clients. One volunteer explained that 'in private practice the client *tells you* what to do because he is paying; clients at the Centre *ask* you what to do'. Most felt it was essential to establish rapport with clients and to win their confidence, and thought this could best be achieved by adopting a relaxed attitude, talking to them in their own terms and using their own language. However one volunteer maintained that he adopted the same attitude as he did in private practice - a more 'pompous' attitude (his term) - since he felt that this was what clients expected of lawyers, and they would feel disappointed if he behaved differently. Another expressed ambivalence on this matter: 'If you're matey then you offend their ideas of what a lawyer should be like; if you become a cool, practical lawyer this attitude defeats the purpose of the law centre.' (15)

As with other groups discussed earlier, there was some divergence of opinion as to the role of the Law Centre. Most saw it as having wide-reaching aims, including education in welfare rights, extending the legal competence of citizens and forging stronger links with community groups for joint action. However, others saw it purely as offering a service based upon the traditional model of a solicitor's office, and felt that in order to do this more efficiently and effectively it was necessary to open additional offices in poor areas and so relieve the strain. It was almost universally held that law centres should be provided on a national basis, funded either through central government or through charitable organizations.

The Centre also relied heavily on day-time volunteers; usually these were law students anxious to gain practical experience whilst studying, but sometimes they were students from other disciplines fulfilling the placement requirements demanded by their courses. They performed a variety of tasks: visiting clients in prison, locating witnesses, delivering briefs, attending court hearings, running errands and occasionally conducting preliminary interviews with clients.

The disadvantage to this system lay in the irregular availability of students. Whereas with the legal volunteers it was possible to insist on regular attendance, the availability of students was dependent upon the university terms and the demands of their courses. Equally there were disadvantages from the students' point of view in so far as the flow of work was spasmodic, and at times there was nothing they could usefully do. This topic was raised at several staff meetings, with the senior solicitor encouraging the full-time staff to make every effort to find them work, or to allow them to sit-in on interviews with clients.

Finally there were also a number of volunteer receptionists who came on a regular basis and took over from the permanent staff in the evenings and at weekends.

STAFF COMMUNICATION

The fact that so many of the staff lived locally and had affiliations with other community organizations in the area often resulted in there being very close informal as well as formal bonds between them. During the research period general staff meetings were in theory held fortnightly, though in practice they took place less frequently, particularly during the summer months when people were away on holiday. Their purpose was to discuss internal administrative arrangements such as the handling of reception, staff appointments and salaries, as well as topics of wider general concern such as future lines of development at the Centre, union membership for staff, and relationships with outside bodies.

In addition to these general meetings, the legal staff met weekly in order to discuss points arising from cases, or the supervision of volunteers, as well as certain wider policy issues which it was hoped to raise with the Lord Chancellor's Advisory Committee on Legal Aid and Advice, or with the newly founded Law Centres' Joint Working Party.

Throughout the research year there was a growing feeling that to have separate meetings was divisive, and it was eventually decided to hold joint meetings on a weekly basis. It was primarily the non-legal staff who pressed for such an arrangement, being anxious to share an even greater sense of involvement in the legal aspects of the Centre's work. (16)

The fact that the total number of salaried staff remained small, and with few changes, meant that a close-knit group could be maintained, and informal networks of communication were relatively effective. However, where an organization has only a small staff, such changes as do occur tend rather easily to upset the balance of relationships. During the research year a new assistant solicitor was appointed, all the secretarial staff changed, a research and development officer, a part-time receptionist and a part-time secretary were added. At one stage the senior solicitor expressed concern at the lack of unity amongst the staff and referred to a 'divisive atmosphere'. Such a view was strengthened when one of the original secretaries, who had left, returned to work part-time and commented that staff morale was very low. (17) In reply one of the lawyers expressed the view that the Centre had expanded, and that it could no longer continue to work 'on the nod' as in the past. However, although it was generally recognized that with new developments the informal networks and mutual trust which had hitherto been adequate would have to give way to more formal methods of communication, no one was really happy with such a solution.

Rather than adopt more formal procedures, an appearance of unity was maintained by alternative techniques. As was suggested earlier, differences of opinion as to goals were not adequately discussed, or if discussed were not satisfactorily resolved for fear of upsetting interpersonal relationships. The solution most frequently adopted was to ask whoever raised a particular issue (and/or its strongest opponent) to prepare a paper for discussion at a later staff meeting. Such a technique served generally to postpone decision-making, since those concerned were already over-stretched in terms of their workload and had little time to set down their views in writing. Two examples may help to clarify this point: the first concerned the continual discussions surrounding the precise nature of the work to be undertaken by the research and development officer. As was pointed out earlier, all were dissatisfied with what was being done, yet no one was willing either to be specific about a job description, or to upset the person concerned by terminating the appointment. This particular issue also provided an interesting example of the way in which attention might be diverted away from the main topic of concern - i.e. the role of the research and development officer - and directed towards allocating blame as between the sub-committee appointed, and members of staff, for the lack of direction and supervision. The second example concerned the extent to which the Centre should adopt a 'political' stance. The member of staff most strongly committed to the view that it should do so never found time to prepare the discussion paper for which everyone was waiting.

SEEKING FUNDS

Without doubt the most significant problem with which the Centre was faced, one which dogged its every step, was that of finance. It was an issue which affected not only the extent to which it was able to carry on its day-to-day work or to expand, but equally the nature of that work and the direction in which it was to develop.

As was mentioned earlier, funds of £9,000 were initially made available to the Centre from two charities over a period of three years. When the Centre opened it operated on a shoe-string budget, making use of second-hand furniture, asking for gifts of books and office equipment, and paying low salaries. This situation has continued and an estimated comparison with a commercial practice given in the Centre's third annual report showed that the Centre was operating at a saving of more than £9,000, the main economy being in salaries and rent (savings of £8,175 and £1,100 respectively). (18)

To operate 'comfortably', without having constantly to be aware of where the next penny was coming from, the Centre claimed to need £40,000 a year, and the minimum sum upon which it could run was said to be £30,000 a year. (19)

The Centre's initial preference for independent financing was primarily the result of an absence of any immediate likelihood of state funding, combined with a fear that local authority funding would be restrictive and would limit the independence of action which the staff considered crucial to many, if not all, aspects of its work. (20)

One aspect of financing in particular was the cause of much concern and considerable disagreement, namely legal aid moneys. (21) By increasing the number of legally aided cases undertaken - particularly criminal work - it was argued by some that the Centre could have become less reliant on other sources of income. However, the staff felt that such a development conflicted with the original goal of the Centre to provide a free legal service to the neighbourhood. An analysis of the 1973 caseload indicated that approximately 60 per cent of the work undertaken was carried out free of charge, and it was argued that any move to increase the amount of legally aided work would severely alter the nature of the whole venture. (22)

Nor were the staff alone in their resistance to increasing the amount of legal aid work: for totally different reasons some members of the legal profession resisted such a move, fearing that if law centres were encouraged to expand in this direction, their own practices would diminish. (23)

The issue of legal aid moneys had yet other ramifications: when appealing for funds from charitable trusts it was necessary to set out the current financial position and to offer a satisfactory - to the funding body - explanation for not relying on high legal aid receipts. Furthermore, towards the latter part of the research period, once legal aid moneys were included in the accounts the Centre appeared, on paper, to be working within its budget. However the figures included 'work in progress' (24) and there was insufficient capital available to cover the time that elapsed before payment could be claimed, let alone be received.

In order to attract funds, alternative strategies were sought which it was believed potential grant-givers would consider attractive because of their innovative nature. These included appeals for money to provide a Mobile Unit, to pay the salary of a research and development officer, and to establish a Housing Unit with research facilities. Such a strategy did not always have the intended results however, and one organization which had in the past supported the Centre for two years, halved its grant when appraised of the fact that the work was to be expanded into the research and development field, fearing that funds earmarked under the terms of the charity for 'the poor of Kensington' might be misused.

Quite early in its history (1971 and 1972) the Centre made two applications to the Home Office for a grant under their Urban Aid Programme, (25) but both were unsuccessful. In order to obtain funds in this way, applications have to be submitted through the local authority who are responsible for a 25 per cent contribution to such a grant and who forward all applications to the Home Office, having first allocated priorities to the various submissions. The Centre's somewhat tenuous relationship with the local authority (culminating in a refusal of funds from that source, see below) may have influenced the negative decisions on the part of the Home Office.

However, the outcome of these difficulties with the local authority was not entirely negative, and following considerable publicity in both the national and local press, the Centre received two anonymous gifts of £10,000 and £3,000 respectively, and an interest free loan of £5,000 was made available from one of the original charities. Despite these injections of money, which enabled the Centre to stay in existence until the end of 1974, the future seemed insecure. By the end of the research period relations with the local authority appeared to have been completely severed and all but one of the original charities had ceased to give financial support having regarded such help as being appropriate only for pilot projects. Even this one continued to provide only on the basis of a loan, and expressed reservations about continuing on any long-term basis. A restricted budget was therefore planned and severe limits placed upon plans for expansion. (26)

ADMINISTRATION

Solicitors at the Centre found themselves in a perpetual dilemma vis-a-vis their workload, being torn between the need to respond to a constantly increasing flow of clients and the need to keep pace with accumulating paperwork. The tendency to concentrate on 'people rather than paper' was, however, a matter of very real concern to the Management Committee and the issue became acute every time there was a financial crisis.

Queries about such matters as legal aid bills, Counsel's fees and even, on occasion, the payment of insurance charges were discussed at both staff and committee meetings, often in the absence of adequate (or accurate) information. In order to deal with the immediate financial problems it became necessary to minimize the amount of case-work undertaken, and on two occasions during the research year no new clients were taken on for a week in order to give time for bills to be rendered, accounts made up, and outstanding moneys collected. Even in strictly financial terms such a solution could not, of course, be regarded as satisfactory; by turning away legally aided clients the Centre was inevitably limiting its future income from this source, since it would thereby be reducing the number of future claims that could be made.

The lack of adequate funds not only limited the number of staff who could be employed, but equally was responsible for determining the type of person available. Even amongst those with a commitment to helping people in need, not all are able or willing, for personal reasons, to work for low salaries. Again, it is sometimes their very commitment which blinds them to the necessity for paying attention to paperwork or keeping adequate records. In the case of the Centre, such filing and recording methods as were used tended to be somewhat individualistic, no recognized system having been adopted overall. This situation undoubtedly arose because the centre grew, like Topsy, in response to immediate and pressing needs, with no one member of staff being given responsibility for office management.

Some eighteen months after the Centre was set up, the Management Committee expressed grave concern about the accounting system, and a full-time book-keeper was then appointed. However, for a long time she was expected to perform a number of additional duties such as ordering stationery, supervising the coffee and xeroxing machines, and similar housekeeping jobs. Furthermore, in cases where the Centre had agreed to act as a rent collecting agent for a client in dispute with his landlord (thereby avoiding the danger of the tenant spending the money and being evicted for non-payment), it was the book-keeper who was charged with the task, one which often involved her in prolonged discussions with clients, bordering on a casework relationship.

Perhaps even more crucial was the fact that even when it was recognized that accounting required her undivided attention, the necessary facilities were not readily available; thus for a long time she was not given a proper office but had to use the kitchen. Only when the financial situation of the Centre became critical was the importance of the book-keeper's work fully appreciated, together with the difficulties under which it was being performed, and an office in the basement was provided.

To some extent these difficulties flowed from the need to restrict expenditure: having previously worked as a ledger clerk, the person appointed as book-keeper was insufficiently experienced to carry out the work unsupervised, but to employ a more qualified person would have meant paying a higher salary. It was thought more advantageous to pay the person concerned a low salary and then pay additional fees to the auditors at the end of the year to sort things out. Such an arrangement might have worked out had there been any one member of staff able to supervise the book-keeping on a regular basis. As it was, the book-keeper had to rely for help on a friendly firm of accountants who happened to have an interest in the work of the Centre and whose services were called upon from time to time. (27)

As problems of administration and finance came increasingly to preoccupy the Management Committee, the appointment of an administrator was discussed on several occasions. Whilst most members of the committee agreed that there was a need for such a person, it was generally recognized that for an administrator to carry out his job successfully he would need to adopt a very firm stance with all the staff and so, by definition, would meet with considerable hostility in an organization which prided itself on a democratic, non-authoritarian approach. A person prepared to face this dilemma was thought to be difficult, if not impossible, to find.

As the heat passed from each crisis, so the question of such an appointment was shelved. At one stage an O and M expert was called in and his recommendation - that there should be regular staff meetings - was eventually implemented though, as was mentioned earlier, it was only rarely that all staff were available at the same time. (28)

Towards the end of the research period a 'volunteer' administrator was approached - someone with business interests and personally known to a member of staff as being anxious to help the Centre in some way. He drafted suggestions for better organization and for the more effective use of office space, and accordingly plans for the latter were due to be implemented.

RELATIONSHIPS WITH THE LOCAL AUTHORITY

In July 1971, after the Centre had been open for about a year, it was approached by the local authority with a view to its becoming a constituent part of a proposed Aid and Information Centre. (29) It was intended that the Aid and Information centre should house a local CAB office, the staff of which would man the reception area, and an area office of the social services department, as well as the local voluntary housing agency. After due consideration the Law Centre turned down the suggestion, mainly because it feared losing its independence and becoming identified with the Town Hall in the eyes of the community it served. In addition there were thought likely to be difficulties in being housed under the same roof as a voluntary organization with which the personnel of the Law Centre had had differences of opinion in the past, feelings which still rankled.

During 1973 the local authority were upset by certain political activities which occurred in the north of the Borough, and which they identified with the Law Centre. Thus they were aggrieved by a broadsheet which referred to Conservative councillors in derogatory terms and which, although produced by another local group, had been displayed along with other items of general information in the Law Centre's window. (30) Even greater resentment was evinced by the Council following a 'lock-in' of councillors in a Church Hall. This event had started as a meeting to consider a Council report on development plans for the area, but feelings of anger amongst local residents and social workers reached such a pitch that representatives of these groups took over the meeting, making specific demands and keeping Council officials in the hall overnight. The story reached the headlines in the national press (31) and the leader of the Council termed those involved 'thugs and anarchists'. Although the Law Centre denied any connection with these activities at the time, a few weeks later the senior solicitor gave an interview to the local press praising the restraint of the police in not moving in on the situation. (32) Needless to say this view was not shared by the leader of the Council and this publicity was thought to have further hardened his attitude towards the Centre.

Reference was made earlier to the Centre's unsuccessful applications for Urban Aid, and in the course of these negotiations some members of the Management Committee felt they had been treated discourteously by the leader of the Council. However, by the summer of 1973 funds were so low that it was estimated that the Centre would have to close on 1 December if no further money was forthcoming, and it was therefore decided to approach the local authority for help, and ask for a sum of £17,500. (33) Whilst fears concerning loss of independence were generally shared, there had always been a number of people, both staff and Management Committee members, who felt that the local authority had a duty to provide funds, and that as long as money from charitable sources continued to be made available, the local authority was able to default on what were regarded as its obligations to the community.

At first the Borough adopted stalling tactics, pointing out that following the Law Centre's refusal to participate in the Aid and Information Centre, some alternative legal provision would need to be made available there, and until this matter had been settled, the Council was not in a position to consider an allocation of funds. Two months later the question was raised at a Council meeting; the leader of the Council publicly acknowledged that the Centre had carried out valuable work and that this would be taken into account when reaching a decision. Eventually, after another month had elapsed, he agreed to meet representatives of the Centre - a step which was viewed by staff and committee members alike as a more positive turn of events.

However, following this meeting the Council refused to make a grant but 'reluctantly' expressed its willingness to consider a loan, *provided that the senior solicitor and two members of the Management Committee ceased to have any association with the Centre.*

The Centre then called a press conference where confidence in the senior solicitor was affirmed, and where it was made clear that the conditions set out by the local authority were totally unacceptable. By the end of the research period there had been no further developments.

RELATIONSHIPS WITH THE LEGAL PROFESSION

Such relationships occurred at three levels: with the Law Society, with the local Law Society, and with individual solicitors. So far as the Law Society was concerned, the Centre was opened by the President of the Society amid general approval, and a member of the local Law Society was appointed to the Management Committee. In addition, all the senior members of that committee had close personal and professional ties with the Law Society and its officers. However, as time went by, the Society's attitude changed somewhat, a situation which may have been related more directly to the setting up of other independently run law centres, rather than to the specific activities of the North Kensington Centre, since such developments could have been interpreted as cutting across the Law Society's wish to set up centres of its own under the Legal Advice and Assistance Act. (34)

In practical terms this change in attitude was demonstrated by the increasing difficulty experienced in obtaining the necessary waivers for newly appointed staff. (35) It was proposed by the Law Society that the regulations be changed, and that all solicitors should give an individual assurance that they would not undertake personal injury work, nor represent 'professional criminals' in court. Previously the Management Committee had been responsible for giving a 'blanket' undertaking to this effect, and both the staff at North Kensington and the Management Committee wished this (more flexible) system to continue. The matter was finally resolved as a result of agreement by the Law Society to consult the Lord Chancellor's Office about the terms upon which waivers would be granted, and the original plan was reverted to.

The fears underlying the demand by the Law Society for individual undertakings must be seen in the context of deteriorating relationships between the Centre and the local Law Society as membership of the committee of that society changed. The main topic of disagreement related to the amount of legal aid work being undertaken, particularly criminal work. It was claimed that private practitioners felt they were losing legally aided clients to the Centre which operated at an advantage by virtue of the publicity it received both locally and through the media. (36)

A further matter of dispute between the Centre and the local Law

Society concerned the feedback of information regarding referrals from the Law Centre to solicitors in private practice. When the Centre was first established it was agreed that the local Law Society should be kept informed of all such referrals (to ensure that the Centre was effectively referring to private practitioners those clients for whom its services were not appropriate), but in practice the relevant lists were not reaching their office. Staff at the Centre declined to accept any blame for this, arguing that it was the responsibility of the Society's own representative on the Management Committee to ensure that lists were forwarded.

Towards the end of the research period a new representative was elected on to the Management Committee by the local Law Society. This arose largely because the previous representative also held the office of chairman, and he became increasingly aware of the conflict of interest inherent in this dual role. The new incumbent held very strong views concerning the 'correct' role of the Law Centre, views which conflicted in large measure with those of the staff and indeed with the majority of Management Committee members. Although he raised these matters repeatedly at committee meetings, by the end of the research period no solution had been arrived at, and relations between the two 'sides' remained tense.

A further attempt to remedy the situation was made by the Law Centre staff who hoped that by sending a representative to meetings of the local Law Society, and having one representative on its legal aid committee, a degree of mutual understanding would be achieved. More recently the Lord Chancellor's decision to lend support to independent law centres, and to help them financially, (37) together with the support of the Law Society, albeit with reservations, may cause the local Law Society to adopt a more conciliatory approach.

In this section we have dealt with the development of the Centre and focused on some of the issues and problems involved. We should perhaps stress that by highlighting these difficulties, there is a danger that a stronger emphasis has been placed on them than is warranted in the context of the total work of the Centre, or in the context of the generally harmonious personal relations existing within the Centre. They were, however, an intrinsic part of its development and specific attitudes and views may be seen, from the examples given, to have influenced the way the Centre was shaped. In particular, the ideology underlying the determination to maintain a democratic structure at times left the decision-making processes very fluid. In organizational terms, this may be thought to have been detrimental to efficiency, yet, to the personnel involved, it was an essential ingredient of the Centre's mode of operation.

Chapter 4

THE CENTRE AT WORK

By February 1971, following six months of work, the Centre was open Monday to Friday, from 9.30 a.m. to 6.00 p.m. and on Saturday from 9.30 a.m. to 1.00 p.m. In addition it was open three evenings a week, one of the full-time solicitors being on duty, assisted by a team of about five volunteers.

In order to provide a twenty-four hour emergency service, the Centre's telephone number was transferred to the home of one of the full-time solicitors after closing hours, and this service was manned at the weekend by a rota of solicitors. (1)

Callers at the office were seen at reception, and once it was established that they needed to see a solicitor, as opposed to dropping in for a minor piece of advice, they were given an appointment to see one of the evening volunteers for a preliminary interview at a time convenient to them, usually the same day or at least during the same week. If the case could be dealt with satisfactorily on a weekly basis, the same volunteer would continue to handle it, under the supervision of the solicitor on duty; in cases of greater urgency, or where a lot of preparation was involved, for example in a court case, it became part of the solicitor's caseload. (2) Emergency cases, such as eviction or persons arrested, were taken directly by the full-time solicitor whose duty day or weekend it was.

From the moment the Centre opened it became overwhelmed with individual cases; (3) this fact, combined with differences of opinion as to the proper role of the Centre has played a crucial part in shaping its development. In the absence of considerable injections of additional cash, the unwillingness of the staff to turn away people who so desperately needed help, and for whom no viable alternative legal service was available, was generally considered to be a legitimate reason for failing to expand in other directions. The Centre's deficiencies were nevertheless recognized by many of those involved; one of the solicitors described its service as a 'legal meals-on-wheels' and a member of the Management Committee referred to it as a 'clinic for the legally injured', both remarks clearly conveying critical overtones regarding the limited nature of the work undertaken by the Centre.

Whilst there was certainly a genuine reluctance to cut down on individual casework, (4) the debate about the 'political' activity of the Centre, (5) probably proved an even greater stumbling block in accounting for the absence of any change in direction. For example, doubts surrounding the appointment of a community worker stemmed to a considerable extent from fears on the part of some members of the Management Committee that the nature of the work to be undertaken by such a worker would involve a concern with issues having strong political connotations, such as group action in the housing field, immigration, community relations, and the enforcement of rights. These were recognized as potential areas of conflict with local or national government, and as such, a threat to the 'non-political' role which it was felt proper that a solicitor should maintain, at least in his professional capacity. (6)

By contrast the staff, in varying degrees, were anxious to see an expansion of their work in these very directions. They felt that by virtue of its position within a community, the Centre was under an obligation to provide more than a solicitor's service, and to participate on a broader front. The general staff attitude appeared to be that it was worth taking the risk of upsetting a few people if the Centre were, by such means, better able to justify its existence vis-à-vis the community. As the senior solicitor commented: 'If the Centre isn't political, then the staff are social workers, and the Centre will be doing the same thing in twenty years' time.' (7)

Towards the end of the research period there were comments from some members of the Management Committee to the effect that the Centre was ceasing to be a dynamic force, and suggesting that it needed recharging with new ideas and new blood. In particular some representatives of community agencies complained that not only had the Centre failed to expand, but it had indeed contracted, since on several occasions it had had to stop taking new clients in order to clear the back-log of paperwork related to existing cases.

Throughout the Centre's history, ideas for expansion have been plentiful and have frequently been discussed by the Management Committee and the staff, but by the end of the research period no real change in direction was in evidence. (8) However, as was mentioned earlier, the revival of the Advisory Council may act as a catalyst in this direction.

THE CASEWORK ROLE OF THE CENTRE

Not all of those who visited the Centre became 'cases', as was noted earlier many called in for general advice - a query over a gas bill, help with filling in a form, how to find a local authority department or even, as did more than one, the address of a local plumber or electrician. Information taken from record sheets kept at reception during 1973 shows a total of 1,052 enquiries, the majority being concerned with housing problems or criminal matters, with matrimonial and family problems being far less frequent though together constituting the next largest group (see Table B.1, Appendix B). (9)

The catchment area covered by the Centre included the four wards of North Kensington and two narrow strips to the east and west of these, giving a total population of over 60,000. (10) Most callers lived within these boundaries, but a substantial number came from outside, some from places as far afield as Manchester, Cardiff, and even Scotland (see Table B.2, Appendix B). (11) It was not always felt by the receptionist to be appropriate to record the source of referral to the Centre when people called, for example if they were too distressed or anxious, or if they found difficulty in answering even the few basic questions necessary. Where such details were recorded, it seems that most clients came through friends or other informal and unofficial sources, though a substantial number were referred by statutory or voluntary welfare agencies, mainly the CAB. A few had heard of the Centre through other sections of the justice system - police, courts, solicitors, etc. (for details see Table B.3, Appendix B).

The Centre did not handle cases for people who neither lived nor worked in the catchment area, nor did it take those cases where it was established that the client could afford to pay a private solicitor. This was initially assessed by the receptionist, usually by the caller's appearance or manner, and subsequently checked at the first interview with a solicitor, by more formal methods; in practice it was very rare that local people were ineligible on this basis. Certain categories of case were also excluded: high court work, divorce or matrimonial cases, commercial or conveyancing work and private prosecutions. Nor did the Centre act for private landlords (12) and after a while it gave up undertaking motoring cases, since these were not felt to come within the boundaries of welfare law and were time consuming.

Reference was made in Chapter 3 to some of the difficulties surrounding the undertaking of criminal legal aid work, in particular the objections raised by solicitors in private practice who feared some loss of work, as well as by the staff of the Centre who felt that legal aid work conflicted with the expressed goal of the Centre to provide a free legal service to the community it served. So far as the former were concerned, the senior solicitor was of the opinion that objections by private solicitors were not nearly so widespread as was sometimes suggested, a view he substantiated by reference to the many messages of support received in times of crisis. Furthermore, he argued that the Centre was bound to have a higher percentage of criminal legal aid cases by virtue of the fact that it offered a 24 hour service, and had built up a good reputation in the area. It was felt by the staff that if there appeared to be any unwillingness to undertake cases when asked to do so, this might legitimately be interpreted by members of the community as a failure to meet an important need for competent legal representation. Finally, it was also suggested to the researcher that the figures relating to legally aided cases might be somewhat distorted by virtue of the fact that the Centre applied for legal aid in all cases, believing from its own experience that it would be granted, whereas private practitioners were thought by the Centre to be hesitant about doing so, fearing that the application would be refused. Furthermore, whilst the Centre claimed payment in every legally aided case, some private practitioners are known not to bother to do so, in order to avoid the extra paperwork involved. (13)

If callers at the Centre were deemed to be able to afford a solicitor, the receptionist would try to recommend one likely to be interested in their particular type of case, the selection being made from a list of solicitors kept by area and type of work specialised in; a person coming from outside the catchment area, and unable to afford to pay, would be referred either to their local law centre - if one existed - or to a private practitioner operating under the Legal Aid Scheme. Failing any of these solutions the receptionist usually recommended that the caller should contact his local CAB for the name of a solicitor.

As was mentioned above, divorce and matrimonial cases were not taken by the Centre; female clients needing such help were referred to a local practice run by a woman solicitor (she only handled cases for women), (14) men being referred to an appropriate lawyer under the Legal Aid Scheme.

Where strictly legal expertise did not seem to be needed, the client was generally referred to an appropriate agency in the community. (15) Table B.4, Appendix B shows details of outgoing referrals for 1973.

THE CLIENTS AND THEIR PROBLEMS (16)

From figures available to the researcher for 1972 and for the first four months of 1973 it was estimated that the Centre handled, or could be expected to handle, approximately 1,500 cases each year, and on this basis it was decided to interview a 10 per cent sample, stratified by type of problem, with a view to ascertaining the clients' views about the Centre and its work. Table 4.1 shows the resultant sample, the figure in brackets indicating the percentage of all such cases handled by the Centre during 1973. (17)

TABLE 4.1 Sample of clients by type of problem

Type of problem	No.	%	% (1973)
Housing	60	40.0	(38.2)
Crime	37*	24.7	(30.1)
Juvenile crime	7	4.7	
All accidents	10	6.7	(4.9)
Consumer	9	6.0	(5.9)
Family	4	2.7	(2.8)
Employment	9	6.0	(4.6)
Miscellaneous	14	9.3	(9.5)
Total	150	100.0	

* Five respondents had been subject to a criminal act, e.g. assault.

A more detailed breakdown of the nature of the 60 housing cases in the sample is set out in Table 4.2, this being the main type of work undertaken by the Centre.

TABLE 4.2 Details of housing cases in sample

Housing cases	No.	%	
Notice to quit	15	25.0	43.3
Possession order	5	8.3	
Threatened eviction	6	10.0	
Query over tenancy agreement/lease	8	13.3	
Harassment	5	8.3	
Repairs	4	6.7	
Arrears of rent	2	3.3	
Increase in rent	2	3.3	
Squatting queries	2	3.3	
Query if tenancy is furnished/unfurnished	3	5.0	
Deposit held by landlord/landlord owes money	3	5.0	
Possessions held by ex-landlady (due to rent arrears)	1	1.7	
Landlady gone abroad with rent book	1	1.7	
Friction with other tenants	2	3.3	
Argument with landlord re: access to garden	1	1.7	
Total	60	100.0	

The fact that security of tenure constituted the major problem associated with housing (43 per cent) was to be expected in a Borough where there is such a high proportion of privately rented accommodation; the 1971 census figures show that Kensington and Chelsea has the highest proportion of privately rented furnished accommodation of all Inner London Boroughs, and takes fourth place with regard to privately rented unfurnished accommodation (see Table 4.3).

Where tenants had been given a notice to quit it was predominantly because the landlord wanted to sell the house (or had already done so and the new owner wanted vacant possession). Many landlords were anxious to renovate property in the area for re-sale at vastly inflated prices, part of a general process of 'gentrification' occurring in a number of Inner London Boroughs.

Demographic information relating to the clients in the sample is given in Tables C.2 and C.3 Appendix C (18) from which it can be noted that those interviewed were predominantly male, (19) aged over 25 and born in London - a sizeable proportion in North Kensington. Most were, or had been, married and worked in skilled or semi-skilled manual occupations (Registrar General categories IIIM and IV).

TABLE 4.3 Inner London Boroughs: Percentages of households in privately rented furnished and unfurnished accommodation

Inner London Boroughs*	Total households	Percentage in privately rented furnished accommodation**	Percentage in privately rented unfurnished accommodation**
Kensington & Chelsea	77,935	38.0 (1)	37.0 (4)
Camden	82,150	26.1 (2)	34.3 (5)
City of Westminster	93,005	25.7 (3)	42.5 (1)
Hammersmith	74,055	21.7 (4)	40.0 (2)
Islington	76,975	19.2 (5)	37.2 (3)
Lambeth	111,940	15.2 (6)	32.9 (7)
Wandsworth	109,835	14.1 (7)	31.7 (8)
Ealing	104,545	13.1 (8)	20.5 (12)
Hackney	79,825	11.3 (9)	33.1 (6)
Lewisham	93,900	6.8 (10)	25.3 (11)
Southwark	93,270	5.7 (11)	30.3 (9)
Tower Hamlets	57,590	3.4 (12)	26.3 (10)

* Excluding City of London
** Figures in brackets show rank order
Source: 1971 Census

Almost one quarter of the clients had been to the Centre on a prior occasion, usually with a housing problem, or one arising out of some criminal activity. The majority had learned of its existence through friends or some other informal contact, but nearly a quarter were referred by another agency. One woman seeking help in connection with a claim for maintenance had previously approached four such agencies, the DHSS, the CAB, the Probation Service and finally her local MP. Perhaps fortunately he was a solicitor who was on the Management Committee of the Law Centre, and so she was referred there.

In choosing to go to the Law Centre rather than elsewhere, the fact that the service was free was clearly a critical factor in the decision, but other reasons mentioned frequently included proximity to home (or work) and the fact that the Centre was open in the evenings. Almost 13 per cent said they went there simply because they badly needed help and did not know where else to turn.

EXPECTATION, OUTCOME AND SATISFACTION

Few clients had any accurate idea of the work undertaken by the Centre, or any clear expectation of the kind of help they either wanted

TABLE 4.4 Type of case by degree of satisfaction

Degree of satisfaction	Type of case									
	Housing		Crime		Juvenile Crime		Accident		Consumer	
	No.	%	No.	%	No.	%	No.	%	No.	%
Completely satisfied	6	(10.0)	5	(13.5)	-	-	-	-	-	-
Satisfied the Centre did everything possible	24	(40.0)	17	(46.0)	6	(85.7)	3	(30.0)	5	(55.6)
Fairly satisfied (although outcome not very satisfactory)	9	(15.0)	5	(13.5)	1	(14.3)	1	(10.0)	-	-
Satisfied so far	5	(8.3)	3	(8.1)	-	-	4	(40.0)	2	(22.2)
Dissatisfied	12	(20.0)	7	(18.9)	-	-	1	(10.0)	2	(22.2)
Only went for advice	4	(6.7)	-	-	-	-	1	(10.0)	-	-
TOTAL	60	100	37	100	7	100	10	100	9	100

Degree of satisfaction	Type of case							
	Family		Employment		Miscellaneous		Total	
	No.	%	No.	%	No.	%	No.	%
Completely satisfied	-	-	2	(22.2)	2	(14.3)	15	(10.0)
Satisfied the Centre did everything possible	4	(100.0)	3	(33.3)	6	(42.9)	68	(45.4)
Fairly satisfied (although outcome not very satisfactory)	-	-	1	(11.1)	2	(14.3)	19	(58) (12.6)
Satisfied so far	-	-	-	-	1	(7.1)	15	(10.0)
Dissatisfied	-	-	1	(11.1)	1	(7.1)	24	(16.0)
Only went for advice	-	-	2	(22.2)	2	(14.3)	9	(6.0)
TOTAL	4	100	9	100	14	100	150	100

or were likely to receive. (20) They simply wanted the Centre to 'sort things out' or 'explain the situation' and they showed a touching faith in the magic powers of the 'professionals' to solve their problems.

Despite the fact that it was called a law centre, only a third thought they would get legal help, a situation which applied largely to those cases involving a court or tribunal appearance. However, even this group evinced some surprise when they discovered that they could be legally represented as distinct from merely being given legal advice.

It was not possible to make any objective assessment of outcome - even of the completed cases. Even under wholly satisfactory research conditions such an exercise presents very considerable difficulties: in North America, for example, attempts have been made to evaluate outcome in terms of lawyer performance using a team of other lawyers as assessors, but results have been of dubious value since there was often disagreement amongst the lawyers as to what could be considered a favourable outcome. (21) No attempt was made to undertake a similar task in the present research, but at the outset it had been hoped that discussions with the solicitors concerned, as well as references to case records, would allow some comparison to be made between the lawyers' assessment of outcome and that of the client. In the event this too proved impossible: the researcher was not allowed access to case files and when the clients were invited to co-operate with the research they were assured by the solicitor that their case would not be discussed with the interviewer by any member of the Centre's staff. Table 4.4 sets out the position as perceived by the client at the time of the research interview. (22)

Since expectations were so ill-defined, it is not surprising that 88 per cent felt that the Centre lived up to their expectations, although only 10 per cent were completely satisfied with the service. Equally unsurprising was the fact that half of those who were not satisfied came from the group who described the outcome of their case as 'unfavourable'.

Over half the sample (58 per cent) believed the Centre had done all it could under the circumstances, and this included two thirds of those who viewed the outcome as negative. The extent of the gratitude expressed by clients was sometimes felt by the lawyers to be acutely embarrassing; they suggested that the type of client who came to the Law Centre was not always sufficiently discerning about standards of service.

DISSATISFACTION

A total of only 16 per cent (24) clients expressed dissatisfaction outright. (23) The main causes for complaint were first, a lack of adequate communication - clients felt they were not kept informed about what was being done, or they had difficulty in reaching the solicitor dealing with their case, or possibly they saw someone else on a subsequent occasion and were told something different. Second, some complained of inefficient administration - for example papers not being sent on time; and third, there were complaints about the fact that someone unfamiliar appeared to represent them in court or at the tribunal, and that this person seemed to have insufficient knowledge of their case.

This last complaint poses a particularly difficult problem: the use of volunteers was an essential feature of the Centre's functioning, as was the use of barristers for certain types of court appearances and in the absence of solicitor-advocates. However it was a situation which undoubtedly had a bewildering effect on clients, particularly if they had not been forewarned, or had failed fully to comprehend the position. Certainly it was an original aim of the Centre to provide a 'friendly representative' who would help demystify court or tribunal proceedings, and it was hoped that the same person would be able to see each case through to the end. In the event this proved impracticable, largely, it was said, because the wide variety of cases undertaken by the Centre necessitated representatives appearing in a large number of widely scattered courts, and consequently being heavily dependent upon outside help. The problems surrounding the use of barristers, some of whom may certainly be inadequately briefed is, of course, one which applies equally to private practice, but in the case of Law Centre clients it is one which may require more explanation, and more careful handling.

The use of volunteers also caused concern at an earlier stage in the client/solicitor relationship. Clients were sometimes left with the impression that the lawyer was not competent to deal with their particular problem, a situation which arose, for example, if the volunteer had to leave the interview room in order to seek advice from the duty solicitor. Clients tended to believe that all solicitors should have the answer to any legal problem at their finger tips, and were dismayed if advice had to be sought from colleagues, or even from books. They had difficulty in appreciating the often complex nature of the problems presented and, of course, were usually unaware that many of the volunteers were normally engaged in work of a totally different nature.

> 'I wanted a more positive statement from them about what my position is. They said of course we don't really know if you're furnished or unfurnished...what I got was opinion rather than fact.... The guy who interviewed me was not at ease and in a position where he had things at his finger tips.'

> 'They referred to books if you asked questions - it should be at the tips of their fingers. If they are dealing with these problems all day they should know them...they were nice people but not competent.'

There were, too, complaints about the hectic atmosphere at the Law Centre and about the long wait that was occasionally involved, 14 of the clients (9 per cent) having been kept waiting for more than an hour for their first appointment. The degree to which clients found waiting irksome depended to a large extent on their individual circumstances: if attendance at the Centre had necessitated taking time off work, or alternatively if they had timed their appointment to fit in with a night shift, they were clearly more likely to be distressed, since delay meant financial loss. Others found the waiting added to the nervous strain at a time when they were already tense and anxious.

Finally there were negative comments about the dilapidated decor of the Centre. Whilst most people sympathized with the staff for having to work in such dismal and overcrowded surroundings, they clearly would have preferred a more cheerful atmosphere, and one client offered to lend a hand with redecorating. (24)

INTENTION TO RETURN TO THE CENTRE

An overwhelming majority (77 per cent) said that they would return to the Law Centre should they need help in the future, and this included 9 per cent who were dissatisfied on the present occasion. However, although 24 of those interviewed admitted to having had a subsequent legal problem, (25) only 6 of them had in fact gone to the Centre about it. A few of the remainder said they had managed alone, but most had gone elsewhere, including child welfare, medical social workers, the police, an insurance company and a private solicitor, often because they knew, or assumed, that the Law Centre would not deal with their particular problem - a claim for personal damges, divorce, or a business matter. (26) Others, who were faced with criminal charges, thought that having committed an offence (27) they must suffer the consequences of their actions, and they did not consider it worth bothering the Centre. One man, on his third charge, felt bad about returning yet again: 'I am frightened to return to the Law Centre. It's as if I was taking liberties by going up there.'

A similar reticence about returning to the Centre was often expressed, in answer to a hypothetical question by those who had not experienced any subsequent legal problem: 'It's not a charity - I couldn't keep going back.'

Five people said that they would consult a solicitor in private practice, believing that it was fairer to do so if one could afford it.

SOLICITOR/CLIENT RELATIONSHIPS

Despite certain anxieties concerning the competence of volunteers to which reference was made earlier, the majority of clients (77 per cent) were satisfied (or satisfied so far) with the service provided, and 94 per cent felt that the lawyer they saw on their first visit was sympathetic to their problem. They experienced little difficulty in making themselves understood, indeed several who did experience this attributed it to their own inarticulateness rather than any failing on the solicitor's part.

As was mentioned earlier, the lawyers themselves often felt that clients were over-generous in their assessment of performance; certainly many clients interviewed seemed to feel that they had no right to question the activities of the lawyer who was acting on their behalf - and this was true even of those who were upset by the lack of information they received. There was a fairly widespread assumption that the solicitor knew what he was doing and should be allowed to carry on.

As many as 41 per cent (61 respondents) of the sample had on a prior occasion consulted a solicitor in private practice, the majority in connection with divorce or matrimonial cases, but a substantial minority had done so over housing problems and in criminal cases. It was generally believed (72 per cent of the total sample) that solicitors in private practice were interested in the same kinds of problems that clients took to the Law Centre, but this included a proportion (17 per cent) who thought that the extent of their interest might depend upon the client's ability to pay.

Most had chosen the Law Centre on this occasion for fear of incurring charges they could ill-afford: only 18 of the 61 had not had to pay anything when they had seen a private solicitor (of whom 14 had received legal aid), many had paid between £50 and £100 and one person claimed to have been charged £2,000 for a criminal case. (28)

Most people described lawyers as well-educated, professional people, 'in it for the money'. They were generally thought to have lower status than doctors (who offer their service as a vocation), but higher status than accountants, estate agents and teachers. References to social class, and a concern with money were frequent as the following comments suggest:

> 'They're business men with an education in the law, they use it to make money and get social position.'

> 'A class above me, out of my circle. I'm just an ordinary man, they're better educated, entitled to get paid more for what they do.'

> 'Upper middle class, not all that rich, but well away from the working class.'

> 'They're members of the golf club with posh accents; they think they're upper class.... Mostly they're interested in making money.'

> 'Business people...the majority are more interested in the fees than in seeing that justice is done to their clients.'

Despite these somewhat pejorative views, no one expressed dissatisfaction with the actual handling of cases by solicitors in private practice, and as mentioned above, most chose the Law Centre purely on financial grounds and for convenience.

For the most part contact with solicitors at the Centre had done little to change their overall views of the profession. This was probably because the kinds of lawyers who worked there were regarded as 'different' from those in private practice. (29) For a few people however the effect was considerable.

> 'The fear has gone out of going to places like that; I would find it easier to go to any solicitor now.'

> 'You can approach them more easily than I expected.'

> 'I feel easier about going to them now and I'd certainly go back to the Law Centre.'

RELATED PROBLEMS

In the earlier discussion of satisfaction it was pointed out that although 77 per cent of clients expressed themselves as 'satisfied' with the Centre, only 10 per cent were completely satisfied. One possible explanation for this may relate to the presence (or absence) of other, related problems and to the extent these were resolved or modified. Earlier work undertaken by the Research Unit had highlighted the fact that legal problems cannot be isolated, and that most of the difficulties people experience contain a social as well as a legal component. (30)

This was overwhelmingly true amongst the Law Centre's clients, at least half of whom suffered from quite serious problems in addition to the one for which they sought help. The majority mentioned financial difficulties, sometimes very severe and accompanied by suicidal feelings. Many were receiving treatment for nervous disorders, and in some cases the effect of the worry had spilled over to family members causing a variety of psychosomatic disorders. Where illness, or a criminal charge, had resulted in a loss of wages and even unemployment, as was often the case, the ensuing financial hardship only served to exacerbate the original problem. In some instances the appalling physical conditions under which clients were expected to live caused health problems, as did the harassment from landlords to which some were subjected:

> 'I couldn't sleep for the constant noise and worry during the day when I was trying to sleep, with the landlord harassing me and deliberately waking me up, saying 'my men are entitled to bang 24 hours a day and there's nothing you can do about it'. I used to dread coming home.'

> 'I suffer from sinusitis which wasn't helped by the hole [in a leaking roof]. They're really emotional problems of not having a place where you can feel secure.'

Perhaps the most extreme repercussions were experienced by a client on a criminal charge who had had to move from his address due to alleged police harassment, and whose children were suffering severe emotional disturbance: 'One child, 5, has begun permanently bed-wetting; the 2 year old became speechless for about 6 months with all this trouble.'

Only about one fifth of those with additional problems said they had mentioned them at the Centre. Those who did so said they mostly received verbal reassurance and were told not to worry (sic). (31) Those who told no one refrained from doing so either because they did not want to bother the lawyers, or because they felt that these other problems were not relevant, having no obviously legal solution. Another fifth said they had sought practical help elsewhere - doctor, or welfare agency, or alternatively they had received moral support from a friend or priest. Whilst it seems likely that this is an underestimate both of help asked for, and help given, it casts doubt upon the wisdom of providing a purely legal service for clients who so clearly experience a wide range of interlocking problems.

The lack of comparative data from other centres, or from private practice, makes it impossible to assess how well the North Kensington Centre compares with other legal services. Nevertheless, despite confusion and disagreement about the role of the Centre and the nature of the work it should undertake, a very considerable amount of legal casework was undertaken before and during the research period, and for this they won the gratitude of a great many clients. In the following chapter the research focuses on the relationship between the Centre and the North Kensington community, with special reference to community knowledge and opinion of its work.

Chapter 5

THE CENTRE AND THE COMMUNITY

THE INDIVIDUAL CLIENT

In an earlier chapter (1) reference was made to the conflicting views surrounding some of the goals of the Centre, and even more surrounding the means of achieving these, but as was then indicated, on one point there was certainly general agreement, namely that the Centre should provide a free legal service to all those living and working in the neighbourhood - it was to form an integral part of the community, working for it and within it. This 'neighbourhood' concept was further reinforced by the importance attached to recruiting staff with local ties and requiring that they should live in the area. (2)

If such a goal were to be achieved, a primary requisite would be a general awareness of the Centre's existence, at least by those living in its catchment area, together with some awareness of the kind of work undertaken. (3) In order to examine these points, 100 local residents who had not used the Centre were interviewed, not only with a view to exploring the extent of their knowledge of the Centre, but equally to find out whether they had experienced problems similar to those of Law Centre clients, and if so what alternative action they had taken.

In demographic terms those interviewed paralleled very closely the sample of clients (see Tables C.2 and C.3, Appendix C). They comprised 44 males and 56 females, mostly married and aged over 25. Nearly half of them were Londoners, 14 per cent having been born in North Kensington, and a large proportion came from the Registrar General's occupational categories III and IV. (4)

To obtain these interviews a random sample of addresses was taken from 100 Law Centre clients and interviewers were asked to call on their next-door neighbour. (5) In this way it was hoped to avoid selecting pockets of the Borough where information about the Centre and its work was limited. Despite this precaution, their knowledge was relatively scant; of the 100 people interviewed, 50 per cent had no knowledge of it at all and a further 14 per cent said that although they had heard of it, they could say nothing about its work. (6) Most of the remaining 30 per cent had only a very vague idea of its activities - 11 per cent of this group mentioned that it gave a free service.

Non-users were presented with a list of potential problems, drawn up to closely parallel those experienced by the sample of clients, and were asked whether they had experienced any of these during the preceding three years and if so what action they had taken. The responses are set out in Table 5.1.

Thus there were 57 occasions where non-users were known to have had problems similar to those experienced by Law Centre clients, yet they neither consulted the Law Centre, nor did they take any alternative action, in fact 14 per cent of them did not know the Law Centre existed. Nothing emerged in the interviews with residents to suggest they differed in any way from the Law Centre clients in their potential for handling their own problems.

Non-users who had sought help were then asked from what source they had done so. Most had approached the person or office they held responsible for the difficulty, for example the DHSS for problems relating to welfare benefits, the tax office, and the landlord or a builder where repairs were involved. Solicitors had been consulted by 12 of the 18 who wanted to make a will, by 3 of the 4 experiencing domestic or marital problems and 7 out of the 12 involved in court proceedings. One other interviewee had consulted a solicitor when his house was broken into. (7)

The degree of satisfaction obtained varied, few clients being entirely satisfied. Most criticisms were of slowness, expense, or the clients' feelings of lack of interest by the solicitor. Nevertheless, with one exception no one had considered taking any alternative course of action, even those who were totally dissatisfied. In that particular instance a woman threatened with a compulsory purchase order had been offered alternative accommodation which she found unacceptable and had then sought advice from the Rent Officer, from the Town Hall, from the GLC and from a solicitor - all to no avail: 'No one can help.'

Finally the interviewees who had not experienced these problems were asked who they would approach (or advise a friend to approach), (8) should they arise in future. Generally speaking respondents were not short of suggestions and the Law Centre was occasionally mentioned. However many expressed a strong feeling that problems are often 'private' or 'personal' and that solutions should not be sought outside the network of family and friends. This was particularly true of elderly people who relied very heavily on sons and daughters for help.

Most frequently mentioned was the CAB - not specifically as a place that helped, but rather as a place from which further information could be obtained: 'They [the CAB] are the only people I've dealt with you see, you go there for anything...'; or 'You have to go to them [the CAB] and they help you; they always help me.' Solicitors were mentioned most frequently in connection with wills (44 out of 82 instances), domestic or marital problems (25 out of 96 instances), accident claims (21 out of 86 instances) and involvement in a court case (61 out of 88 instances). (9)

A total of 54 per cent of non-users had at some time in their lives consulted a solicitor (10) compared with 41 per cent of Law Centre clients (see pp.40f). Fourteen per cent had done so in connection with criminal matters, 11 per cent in respect of conveyancing, 11 per cent regarding accident claims, 8 per cent concern-

TABLE 5.1 Incidence of problems experienced by non-users

Problem	Whether help sought			
	Experienced and no help sought	Experienced and help sought	Not experienced	Total
Difficult forms to fill in, e.g. income tax return	8	18	74	100
Wanting to make out a will	5	13	82	100
Repairs to house/flat that were left undone	9	24	67	100
Trouble from neighbours, e.g. noise	12	10	78	100
Problems claiming welfare benefits, e.g. sickness, unemployment	3	17	80	100
A rent increase you thought unfair	8	12	80	100
Any accident, e.g. at work, in the street, where you might have wanted to take action against the firm or another person	3	11	86	100
Problems at work concerning e.g. back pay, holiday money	1	2	97	100

Problem	Whether help sought			
	Experienced and no help sought	Experienced and help sought	Not experienced	Total
Your landlord threatened to turn you out (or loss of home due to redevelopment)	-	11	89	100
Any domestic problems or problems in your marriage	1	3	96	100
Difficulties in paying HP instalments (or any debts)	5	2	93	100
Involvement in a court case, including county court (other than as a witness or a juror)	2	10	88	100
Any other problems, e.g. consumer problems	-	10	90	100
Total	57 (4.4%)	143 (11.0%)	1100 (84.6%)	1300

N = 100, therefore numbers = percentages

ing housing other than conveyancing, 8 per cent regarding divorce or matrimonial problems, and 8 per cent in connection with making a will.

THE USE OF SOLICITORS

When those who had never consulted a solicitor were asked to think of any matters about which they might consider doing so (other than the problems listed above) 36 per cent could think of nothing: 'These would not be for me unless I won the pools'; 'Not for the likes of this class around here; they can't afford the rates'; 'Solicitors cost too much money for people like us. Rich people can get them - not people in this area'; 'I wouldn't go to a solicitor - couldn't get one and it would cost too much. I couldn't speak to him'. Thirty four per cent mentioned conveyancing or 'anything involving big amounts of money', but for the most part their views were rather vague: 'a serious problem' or 'something really bad'; usually this meant a criminal charge or a court appearance. Several people mentioned that if they had to see a solicitor they would opt for 'a Poor Man's Lawyer', provided they could find one.

Interviewees were asked how they had located a solicitor or how they would do so should the need arise. Those who had already used a solicitor had usually heard the name through a relative or friend, seven had been recommended to one through the CAB and five had simply seen the firm's name outside the door and had walked in. Amongst non-users, most thought they would ask amongst their friends (26 per cent) but almost as many said they would rely on seeing a name plate outside the office. Eight people said that they would look in a telephone directory (i.e. classified) and six thought the CAB would be able to provide a name.

KNOWLEDGE OF LEGAL AID (11)

Although it has been emphasized throughout this report that only a very limited range of problems was defined by those who experienced them as 'legal', it may be argued that in approaching a centre designated as a law centre, people might view it specifically as an alternative to legal aid. Under such circumstances they might consult the Centre only after having tried to obtain legal aid and assistance.

Over two thirds of the Centre's clients claimed to know something about the Legal Aid and Advice Scheme, but when asked to explain it, only about a third of these were able to give anything like a comprehensible explanation, and most had only a very rough idea of how the scheme worked. A few went so far as to suggest that legal aid was a place to go to, or that it was synonymous with the Law Centre. Amongst non-users even fewer knew much about it, only 10 per cent giving a reasonably coherent explanation and, as with clients, as many as a third having no knowledge at all. Nor did previous contact with a solicitor in private practice appear to make any difference for either group; of the 54 per cent of non-users who had consulted a solicitor, 13 per cent had actually received legal aid, and in the client group 9 per cent mentioned receiving it.

Although at the time of the interviews a national publicity campaign was launched by the government to publicize 'New Legal Aid' and the introduction of the £25 scheme, using newspapers and television, very few indeed of either group could give the barest details of what the scheme involved. (12)

VIEWS ABOUT THE LAW AND THE LEGAL SYSTEM

In considering the use made of the Law Centre it may be useful to bear in mind the broader perspective from which clients or potential clients view the legal system, (13) and in particular the degree to which they regard it as a just and legitimate system. If people regard the law, and not merely lawyers, as being for 'them' and not for 'us' it is likely that feelings of alienation will prevent the use of any service. Recognizing a problem as a legal one does not necessarily mean that a person is willing to take action, indeed he is unlikely to do so if he feels fatalistic about the outcome.

The findings of the Unit's pilot study dealing with these issues have been reported elsewhere (14) and they were confirmed in the present study of the North Kensington community. They can be summarized in a few words: people took a somewhat traditional view of the law (15) and it was generally seen as fair, albeit favouring property rights. However the legal system - the means by which laws are enforced, and the administration of justice, were generally regarded as grossly unfair. In particular it was repeatedly stressed that money was the nub of the matter - with it one could afford to buy better advice or representation than could be obtained under the Legal Aid Scheme, and in court proceedings it enabled one to bribe police or witnesses. 'They were very rude because I was on legal aid. The magistrate said "Oh God, not another one off Government money" - I'll never go back I hope.'

Similar views affected the decision as to whether or not to use a solicitor. As was pointed out earlier, clients referred to lawyers' over-riding concern with making money, often, it was felt, at the expense of other people's troubles. This view was widespread amongst both those who had, and those who had not, consulted a lawyer at some time; 39 per cent of all those who had never consulted a solicitor felt this way.

So far as the courts were concerned, those interviewed regarded them as a last resort. The burden of their criticism fell upon their disregard for the individual person and his circumstances. Only those able to exert influence through their wealth or education received justice - ordinary working-class people felt themselves to be engulfed by the rigours of the legal process and by its mystification. 'I feel that if I went to court I'd be treated like one of the herd - they've got no time to be personal.' In so far as their appearance or life-style diverged from the middle-class values of those administering the system, they were unlikely to be understood or treated sympathetically.

'X *[mentioning a well-known MP]* got his costs, nobody else did. It's all political - in keeping with capitalism - the law is to protect property and so excludes most of the community. It's

> there for the convenience of a moneyed society - it only helps people with money.'
>
> 'There has never been a successful campaign to introduce working class people to the bench, therefore you get middle-class values introduced in the courts so even when they think they're administering justice, in my opinion they're not. There was a recent example of a central heating engineer who appeared in court in overalls as a witness - he was asked to go home and change into proper clothing.'

COMMUNITY AGENCIES

The material in this section was collected during the research year partly by informal discussions with staff of other agencies, but mainly from twelve interviews with staff of voluntary agencies (16) in the area who both used the Centre for referrals and to whom the Centre in turn referred cases.

Relations between the Centre and most agencies in the area, both voluntary and statutory, were reasonably good and workers expressed satisfaction that they were able to get legal advice over small matters very quickly. They viewed with dismay the possibility of the Centre having to close for lack of funds.

Initially the police had shown some suspicion of its work, particularly as they were unused to solicitors visiting their clients at the police station at all times of the day or night. Nevertheless the staff of the Centre believe that the effect of this emergency service reduced the amount of 'verbals' and physical violence which those detained in police stations were sometimes thought to experience. Over time, relations with the police have improved, despite occasional difficulties between the Centre's staff and particular individuals in the force, often newcomers to the area, and for the most part solicitors have been granted the facilities they asked for; indeed on occasion the police themselves refer clients to the Centre. (17) Nor have the staff been slow to take up allegations of maltreatment or misconduct on behalf of clients, and this may have had a sobering effect in an area where police/community relations were not known for their harmony. (18) In addition, the Law Centre started to keep a police file, taking note of cases in which a police officer was involved and commenting on his conduct in the case.

There was a good deal of interchange of clients between the Centre and voluntary agencies in the community, predominantly in relation to housing cases, but quite frequently in connection with social welfare benefits or immigration problems. For the most part all such work was carried out on a one-to-one basis, but occasionally the Centre co-operated in a group case, as for example when, together with a voluntary housing agency, they persuaded a group of immigrant families to form a club which then met weekly to discuss their problems with staff from the two agencies with a view to their pooling their resources in order to assist and support the immigrant families.

Another example of group activity concerned a joint attempt with a housing agency to persuade tenants to press for their rights in relation to housing repairs. Tenants were notified of the facilities available and provided with pro-forma letters to complete and return to the Public Health Department of the local authority.

However such group cases were relatively unusual and were confined to advising and helping; so far as is known there were no examples of the Centre representing agencies or organizations.

The statutory services were generally used by the Centre as agencies to which clients could be referred, (19) although occasionally the solicitors put pressure on the social services department to ensure that clients' rights in respect of practical help were protected, and help made available under existing legislation.

The local authority housing department was mainly used by the Centre for getting clients on to the housing list. Occasionally the Tenancy Relations Officer was referred to in respect of neighbour disputes, but the Centre made it their policy to avoid involvement in cases of that nature, feeling that it should not take action on behalf of one tenant (member of the community) against another. Such an attitude would seem to reflect the basically traditional approach to conflict resolution which remained the key feature of the Law Centre; it could not easily adapt to the role of mediator, being more concerned to 'take instructions' from clients.

AGENCY CRITICISM OF THE CENTRE

Most of the long-established and more traditional voluntary agencies saw the Centre's primary function as offering a solicitor's service to the community. They viewed with some alarm any suggestion that it might become more radical in its approach and it was said that such a change in direction would be harmful to the Centre's image and would not be in keeping with its original aims and terms of reference. (20)

Such views were not shared, however, by some of the more innovative voluntary groups in the community who were often quite vocal in their criticisms. Whilst they agreed that a casework role gave credibility to the Centre, they expected that law reform would be a natural extension of any such work, the two functions being complementary.

Two groups went much further than this and protested at the conventional role played by the Centre, whereby the traditional lawyer/client relationship was maintained even when the solicitor was acting on behalf of groups of clients. It was thought that by acting as mediator between the client and the legal system the Centre was both supporting the status quo and protecting the professionalism of solicitors. (21) In their view the Centre should adopt a more aggressive role by developing the legal competence of clients, by stimulating community organizations, by encouraging the use of McKenzie men, (22) and by demystifying the law to the advantage of the man in the street, rather than upholding it and acting as mediator. Two examples may help to illustrate this point: on one occasion the Centre was criticized for not giving sufficiently active support, and for failing to carry out the necessary legal research, in connection with a move to get a row of houses taken into public ownership following a long period of what was felt to be mismanagement by successive private landlords. On a second occasion the Centre was criticized for not taking the necessary initiative by representing tenants in respect of their alleged right to be rehoused, as a result of considerable hardship and suffering following major redevelopment of the area.

In cases of this type, the staff of the Centre were felt by some agencies to be failing in the essential task of reaching out into the community and helping individuals and groups to clarify their interests and goals, and then setting about helping them to achieve these.

Some individual welfare workers who had spent many years working in this particular community were concerned about the changes they felt had taken place in the type of clients using the Centre. It was suggested that it had gradually come to be viewed by the traditional working-class community as a Centre which helped 'hippies', those involved in the drug scene and black people. As a consequence they were themselves reluctant to use the Centre, partly through not wishing to identify themselves with those considered 'marginal' in society and partly because they feared the Centre would not be interested in their more 'traditional' problems. This feeling was said to extend to the stall holders in the market lining the street outside the Centre, and it was observed that as a group these stall holders refused to sign a petition in support of the Centre when it was feared that financial difficulties would force it to close.

Several welfare workers mentioned feeling that because the Centre was staffed in the main by young people, this would be off-putting to older people in the community. In practice this seemed not to be true since 37 per cent of the client sample were aged 60 and over.

Relations with the black community in the area were mixed; certainly observation suggested that the Centre dealt with a large number of black clients, (23) but relations with the more radical elements in the black community were tenuous. The Law Centre was criticized by them on much the same grounds as the more radical white groups (see above), namely, their evolutionary, reformist style of work as opposed to a, for them more desirable, revolutionary, radical style. However it was noted that when such critics themselves came into conflict with the law they would immediately contact the Law Centre for help. Even so the relationship was not always an easy one - black clients from these groups tended to be on the defensive and as a result were sometimes abrupt and abrasive in their dealings with staff, and the staff, in turn, were wary of such clients fearing that if crossed they might take violent action against the premises. (24)

THE 'COMMUNITY' OF LAW CENTRES

During the research period a number of new law centres opened their doors, the majority of them in the London area and a Law Centres' Working Group was set up in order to provide a forum for the discussion of common problems, and to thrash out policies.

The relationship between these newer centres and North Kensington was not always an easy one; whilst there was a general feeling that the three years' pioneering work done by North Kensington had paved the way for the smooth operation of the newer centres, there were also doubts about the wisdom of following too closely the policies underlying their work. Indeed most of the North Kensington staff themselves felt that the centres should be 'loosely associated' rather than 'closely affiliated' and regarded it as more important that the policy of each centre should reflect the specific needs of its own neighbourhood rather than forging links one with the other.

The picture is a confused one; initially the staff of the North Kensington Centre appeared to feel that other centres would prove less satisfactory because the people working in them were usually recruited from outside the area and were therefore thought to lack the grass roots attachment which the staff at North Kensington felt to be so crucial. Yet in practice it has been in some of these other centres that community workers have been employed, apparently with considerable success, a situation which has undoubtedly lent weight to those members of the North Kensington staff and Advisory Council who would wish to see that Centre approach its work from a new, community-oriented, perspective. This is exemplified by reference to their latest annual report (1974) in which they state:

> Hitherto the Law Centre has operated an open-door policy but it is felt that we should perhaps be more selective in the type of case we do. It is thought that perhaps a more effective way of operating might be to concentrate on a particular street or a particular problem and with this in mind we are now acting for a group of council tenants...whose flats have fallen into disrepair...a lot of work is required which will mean putting aside some of our more routine work. It is felt to be important, however, since if actions are successful it may well improve the lot of all council tenants in North Kensington.

Such a comment presumably implies that a more selective approach would provide the necessary time to pursue community work.

But disagreements regarding day-to-day administration, or even more fundamental issues of policy, have not prevented the law centres from presenting a united front whenever they felt threatened by outside intervention. Reference was made earlier to the problems experienced at North Kensington in relation to the granting of waivers by the Law Society, an issue the importance of which escalated as the number of law centres increased. Similar difficulties arose later in connection with the employment of articled clerks - it being suggested by the Law Society that law centres did not provide them with 'suitable' experience. (25) An even more disconcerting event for the law centres, and one upon which they were united in opposition, was the publication of the 22nd Report of the Law Society which, in its report to the Lord Chancellor expressed concern about the way in which voluntary law centres were proliferating, and bearing a suggestion that the use of public funds was not being properly safeguarded:

> The Council [of the Law Society] wish to draw attention to certain matters which have caused them some concern. It was inevitable that the delay between the publication of the proposals for the extension of the Legal Aid and Advice Scheme, their substantial embodiment in a Bill and ultimate implementation under an Act should have encouraged the launching of a number of volunteer, charitably based ventures designed to fill the gaps left by the

national Legal Aid and Advice Schemes and to anticipate the measures contained in the new Act. The evidence of the great concern shown by so many, and the reservoir of enthusiasm this has revealed, is a matter for satisfaction; but it carries with it the danger of a fragmentation of effort and resources which, even though it will provide useful indications of the lines upon which legal aid and advice in England ought to develop, could produce a confusion that would retard the gaining of the objectives aimed at. The Council take the view that monies derived from public funds should not be scattered amongst differing legal aid enterprises subject to divergent controls and with differences in the scope of the legal services provided.

Whilst there have been differences of opinion with regard to the funding of law centres as between North Kensington and other centres, several of whom are supported by substantial contributions from their local authority, none would accept the criticism of potential misuse of public funds which it was thought was implied in the Law Society's statement quoted above. At the time of writing, the Law Centre's Working Group is supporting the Legal Action Group's proposal (26) for a Legal Services Commission which would take over responsibility for both the civil and criminal Legal Aid Schemes, including overall planning and policy direction, and which would administer both area and local schemes through a network of Area Legal Services Councils; the two schemes would need to share the present adjudication machinery for Legal Aid applications, the existing area committees perhaps becoming sub-committees of the new Area Legal Services Councils. In addition block grants would be available to law centres, the area councils would be responsible for seeing that neighbourhood law centres were set up where a need became apparent, or those interested in setting up such centres could apply to the commission for such a grant.

From a funding point of view a block grant would certainly be welcomed by those connected with the North Kensington Law Centre, but the setting up of a commission is not likely to be received favourably by at least one member of the Management Committee who would deplore any move to loosen the ties with the Law Society at both national and local level.

Chapter 6

WHERE NEXT?

The move to set up law centres in this country undoubtedly represented an attempt by a group of 'concerned' lawyers and others to make the legal system work more efficiently and at the same time more economically in the interests of social justice. In so doing they were clearly influenced by North American experience, whereby the Economic Opportunity Act of 1964, which initially provided for the Federal funding of community action programmes, was quite rapidly extended to include legal services. It would, however, be quite misleading to draw too close a comparison between the two situations: in the USA the neighbourhood law offices developed as 'a means of providing the opportunity, the orientation and the training to stimulate self-reliance and leadership amongst the ranks of the poor'. (1) These goals were to be achieved by four means: community education, law reform, community action and participation of the poor.

No such goals were adumbrated for centres in this country either in the pages of 'Justice for All', or in the records of discussions which preceded the setting up of the first of such centres - in North Kensington. The aim was to provide a professional service capable of bringing 'high quality legal services to those parts of our cities where the existing need is greatest, and of attracting men of ability to the service of the community'. (2) No mention was made of law reform, community action, or participation of the poor; the emphasis lay upon offering a service to the community, upon 'extending to those now denied it the benefits associated with the tradition of the family solicitor'. (3) It was believed that this goal could be achieved by a major reorganization of the administrative structure, and an increase and reallocation of scarce resources; no radical overhaul of the system was thought to be needed. Indeed in the words of 'Justice for All': 'It is central to the proposal for local legal centres that they should operate by way of *extension not incursion upon, the existing arrangements of the legal aid and advice scheme...*' (our italics). Furthermore the pages of the pamphlet were filled with words of reassurance aimed at mollifying those private practitioners who feared that the introduction of a salaried service - albeit on such a limited scale - would result in a loss of work. Thus not only were a whole range of issues to be excluded from the caseload of projected law centres, but equally it was explained that their existence would generate new work for the private sector. At that time the American concern with social change was nowhere reflected in new plans for the delivery of legal services in this country.

Over the past three years many of those lawyers most directly concerned with developments in the field, together with some of their academic colleagues and with sociologists, social workers and social administrators, have become increasingly aware that the issue of meeting legal need is more complex than had at first been thought. Whilst the overlapping nature of legal and social need is now quite generally recognized, (4) this was by no means always the case. In their memorandum of 1968 the Law Society clearly envisaged differentiating between the two kinds of need, recommending that lawyers should not concern themselves with those aspects of cases which they claimed were more appropriately the concern of social welfare agencies. The role of the proposed liaison officers was to include differentiating between these types of need and referring clients accordingly. (5)

In recent years the solution most frequently put forward is the adoption of a multi-disciplinary approach: it is argued that if lawyers, social workers, and community workers would only pool their resources, the problems faced by the underprivileged would be viewed from a wider perspective, legal services would no longer be isolated, and community action programmes could be initiated. (6) Although such a move indicates a slight shift in goals, the means proposed for their achievement remain much the same as those set out in the early days of the law centre movement, namely helping individual clients, albeit by a team approach. A nod is made in the direction of the social change lobby in so far as legal skills are to be extended towards the aim of educating the community about their rights, and helping them to assert these rights, either on an individual basis, or by the promotion of local organizations; but no shift in power is envisaged, this is to be retained by the professionals offering the service.

More recently still there has been pressure, mainly from within the law centre movement itself, for a legal services programme concentrating heavily on social change, to be achieved by helping the poor community to develop economic and political power. The means by which it is proposed that such a goal should be achieved is the involvement of the indigenous working-class population of a neighbourhood in the control and day-to-day administration of the legal services programme, as well as much more active 'political' involvement by the staff of the programme.

It seems that little attention has been paid to the lack of success attributed to attempts at 'participation of the poor' in the USA. So far as many of the OEO programmes were concerned, such participation was considered as an 'unnecessary evil accompanying OEO funds' and so was either largely ignored, or acknowledged only with reluctance. (7) Strategies adopted seem very similar to those used at North Kensington; either a separate advisory committee composed of local residents was set up in the hope that this would ensure participation, the real power being nevertheless retained by the Management Committee, or alternatively it was community 'leaders' (teachers, clergy, voluntary workers, etc.) who sat on the controlling body, rather than ordinary residents. Carlin has gone further, inasmuch as he questions the viability of the twin goals of control by the client and social change. He claims that an analysis of one major programme in America indicated that measures adopted to achieve institutional change were frequently ineffective unless combined with the mobilization of political support in the middle-class as well as in poverty communities. (8)

At present we have in this country three 'models' of a law centre:

'A' A salaried legal service which extends to the poor community a traditional service similar in structure to that provided to middle-class clients by private practitioners. Needs are defined by the clients, in response to what they see as the type of service offered. Management and control are vested in the [predominantly] legal staff, jointly with representatives of community agencies.

'B' A multi-disciplinary service in which the skills of the lawyers are made available to the community, either on an individual or a group basis. Needs are defined partly by the clients and partly by the staff of the Centre. Management and control are vested in the staff, jointly with representatives of community organizations.

'C' A comprehensive service in which the skills of a wide variety of professional workers are placed at the disposal of the community. The community is encouraged to articulate its own needs and by the development of co-operative self-help, to act to meet these needs. Management and control are vested in the local residents.

Reference to the research at North Kensington suggests that up to the time the research ended, the Centre presented in microcosm the dilemma of the legal services controversy as it is currently seen in these three models. The centre at North Kensington was set up in accordance with model 'A' and the service provided has remained almost exclusively upon the adoption of a professional posture vis-à-vis individual clients. Although professional advice has readily been made available to community groups and organizations, there has been a reluctance to become at all closely involved in what may be interpreted (very widely) as 'political' activities, and even law reform and community education have been largely eschewed.

It is important to recognize that in adopting such a position, the Centre was clearly responding to the demands of almost all sectors of the community. The residents of North Kensington held very traditional views about the role of lawyers and of the nature of the service provided by the Centre. Those who became its clients were almost unanimous in their expressions of gratitude and satisfaction. The legal profession was content to allow the Centre to continue its work undisturbed, provided the staff neither undertook cases that would otherwise go to private practice, nor damaged the image of the profession by their activities. Even those who were most critical of its work - representatives of the more radical movements in the community - believed that the legal service offered to individual clients provided the basis for establishing the Centre's credibility in the eyes of the community.

Furthermore, a number of both internal and external constraints contributed to the perpetuation of such a largely individualized service. In the first place the recurrent financial crises at the Centre were functional, in so far as the fight for survival provided frequent opportunities for all shades of opinion to unite, and ideological differences tended to lose their immediacy. A second factor also contributed to the dampening of ideological debate, namely the lack of clear leadership. Much time was spent in discussion but unless one member of a group can clearly command sufficient support to carry through changes in policy, there will always be a tendency to perpetuate the status quo. Third, the sheer burden of the ever-increasing caseload meant that no one had the time nor the energy to devote to the development of alternative strategies, nor even to convince opponents that new approaches might be desirable. (9) Fourth (and the list is by no means intended to be comprehensive), the absence of any alternative types of professional competence in the Centre meant that other kinds of work such as legal research, law reform, community development, welfare rights education and so forth were either neglected, or carried out with only limited proficiency.

In practice the strategies adopted by this and other law centres in this country have not fallen clearly within the parameters of any one of the three models described above. The service offered has for the most part included aspects of all of them, only the emphasis has differed. This may be because, as mentioned earlier, the answer to the isolation of the legal profession has been seen in terms of a multi-disciplinary approach, one which involved not so much 'team-work' as 'interchangeability'. In other words the nearer the solution sought approaches model 'C', the more closely are the roles of all those employed by the centre (including clerical staff) regarded as virtually interchangeable. Furthermore, there is in some instances an implicit assumption that to be effective the staff must identify closely with the community they serve, an assumption which seems to go beyond the need to have an understanding and appreciation of the values held by that community.

It could be argued that recognition of the social as well as the legal nature of the problems experienced by those in low-income groups does not require such a blurring of roles, but rather a redefinition and an extension of the legal role of the lawyer. This would not mean abandoning the goal of social change, but the transfer of economic and political power which is sought would be achieved by the lawyers using exclusively legal skills to assert the rights of the underprivileged. This the lawyer is ideally placed to do, both by virtue of his training in client-centred advocacy, and by his knowledge of the law which enables him to ensure that those currently exerting power are not able to abuse it by some technicality or infringement of the regulations. The extent to which lawyers working in a particular law centre achieve this end will depend largely upon the issues which they choose to represent. This, in turn, will depend upon the degree to which they choose to convert the needs of the poor (as articulated by the poor) from 'privileges' to 'rights': 'The poor have rights that the majority must recognise even if it is not feeling generous, and even if its larger economic goals are not served thereby.' (10) At the same time it must be recognized that it is not simply a matter of the choice made by lawyers; they may well be willing and able to represent clients in new ways and so contribute to the resolution of their problems, but unless they also devote a considerable part of their time to studying the adequacy of existing law and legal institutions, the solutions they offer will remain circumscribed by today's legislation as well as by current procedures.

It may be said that any solution which calls for an extension of the professional skills of the lawyer will serve only to further mystify the law, and so prevent self-help movements from developing their own legal competence. However, by using law to assert rights in contexts which at first sight appear to be non-legal, there is likely to be a growing awareness amongst those helped that the law can indeed be used for their benefit, and that it does not act exclusively to the advantage of the rich. Equally importantly, law reform, the opening up of new areas of law, and new techniques for applying it, may all bring about important changes in the training of lawyers and in the attitudes of the legal profession.

In the long-run, however, any consideration of the future organization of law centres in this country demands that policy-makers should first make explicit the social ideologies upon which they plan to proceed. (11) Once that has been articulated, it should be possible to decide upon the goals which centres are intended to achieve, since such goals will quite clearly affect the way the service is to be organized. (12) At the same time it needs to be recognized that the contrary argument is also true; the way a service is organized will to a large extent determine the clientele it serves and, in responding to their needs, the goals it achieves.

If funding is to be made available from government sources, the question undoubtedly arises as to the degree to which law centres will be free to work towards the promotion of social change, in so far as this means any real transfer of power. And this leads to a further consideration: in this country plans for the restructuring of legal services have concentrated almost exclusively on provisions for poor people. With the increasing costs of legal services - and in particular litigation - many middle-class clients simply cannot afford the protection of the legal system. (13) In seeking such protection, however, it is unlikely that they envisage becoming involved in a system which is designed to bring about major social change - at least not in the context of resolving their particular legal problems. (14) Is there then to be a dual service, one which caters for poor people and which involves a political commitment to social change and prevention, and another catering for those in the middle-income group through such means as an extension of the legal aid scheme, legal service insurance, or group legal services? (15) Or are we moving slowly but unmistakably in the direction of a national legal service, one which accommodates both strands, and in which the extension of legal competence through education, legal research, and law reform all form an integral part of the service offered?

Chapter 7

A BRIEF SUMMARY

In the introduction to this book, the reasons for presenting the material as a case-study were explained. A major disadvantage to using such an approach lies in the fact that intensive evaluation may lead to undue emphasis being laid on certain aspects of the work which, had more comparative data been available, might have assumed less significance. This situation is further compounded by any attempt to summarize the findings. Both these points should be borne in mind when reading this section.

The concept of Neighbourhood Law Centres developed as one potential response to the growing dissatisfaction with the workings of the 1949 Legal Aid and Advice Act. The full implementation of this Act had been subject to considerable delays, in particular there had been a heavy concentration on those sections of the Act relating to litigation, and the provisions relating to legal advice had been largely set aside.

Increasing recognition of the unmet need for legal services in England coincided with developments in the USA where concern about urban poverty and deprivation led, in 1960, to the passing of the Economic Opportunity Act. The provisions of this Act were extended to include widespread government funding for Neighbourhood Law Offices and the experiences of these offices further encouraged similar developments in England.

It would, however, be unwise to draw too close a comparison between the two situations; whereas in the USA legal services were seen as part of the much wider 'war on poverty', in England the aim at that time was a more modest one, namely to provide a professional service to those who did not normally have access to the legal profession.

The North Kensington Law Centre, the first to be established in England, opened in a traditionally working-class area of London, well known for its poor social conditions. Many of those who pioneered the Centre were already working there as lawyers, social workers or community workers, often in a voluntary capacity, and they were particularly dismayed at the absence of any adequate legal expertise.

In the early days the enthusiasm with which the Management Committee and the staff viewed the potential of the Centre in terms of its day-to-day work with clients, resulted in very limited consideration being given to its structural organization and administration. In particular it was not sufficiently well recognized that the differing backgrounds and professional skills of those involved would inevitably mean that there would be differing expectations concerning the goals of the Centre. About this there were differences of opinion not only between the staff and the Management Committee, but between the staff themselves. Whilst there was agreement that the primary role of the Centre should be to make a lawyer's service available to those not normally having such access, there was less agreement as to what ends those services were intended to achieve, and hence differing views about the means of achieving them. Essentially the dichotomy lay between those who wished to concentrate upon a casework function, and those who believed that the law should be used as a resource, a means of promoting social change. In practical terms the significance of these differences lay in the problems they created when attempting to reach decisions about the professional background and training of the staff to be employed, the nature of the work they would undertake, and the way in which the very scarce financial resources available were to be allocated.

On one matter the staff were, however, virtually unanimous, namely that the Centre should be run on truly democratic lines, and that a hierarchical system of administration should be avoided. As a result, there was no clearly articulated 'staff' view which could be presented to the Management Committee, nor anyone prepared to speak for all. Many members of that committee found it difficult to make the kinds of policy decisions which they felt it incumbent upon them to make, on the basis of what appeared to them to be conflicting and often confused advice, from those most intimately concerned in the running of the Centre.

It may be argued that had there been more effective planning, many of the controversies which arose might have been avoided and it is of course very difficult to assess their effect on the casework function of the Centre. To some extent they were undoubtedly counter-productive since a great deal of time and energy was spent at meetings trying to clarify policy and to resolve administrative problems. Possibly the solution lay in having a democratic form of administration for the legal or casework function of the Centre, whilst at the same time reserving a more authoritarian structure for its routine activities. Such a solution would, however, have required that the senior solicitor be prepared to play both roles (unlikely in the present context), or alternatively that an administrator or office manager be employed, a situation which would probably have been untenable given the ideological commitment of the staff to democracy. Certainly the issues being debated during those early days at North Kensington were later to inform the discussions which culminated in the opening of other centres run on somewhat different lines in other parts of London. The development of their policies and strategies undoubtedly benefited from the experience of North Kensington.

Throughout the history of the Centre, these internal constraints were, however, largely obscured by one overwhelming external constraint, namely the lack of funds. This was crucial in so far as it both hindered plans for expansion and prevented adequate consideration being given to alternative methods of working. Furthermore, it diverted the energy of the staff from the day-to-day casework as, for example, when the Centre had to stop taking clients in order to catch up with paperwork, and so retrieve all possible moneys owing to them from the Legal Aid Fund. Finance, or rather the lack of it, could also be considered dysfunctional in that discussions on this topic often dominated Management Committee meetings and overshadowed debate on broad issues of policy.

The shortage of funds has to be seen in the context of another external constraint; from the moment the Centre opened it became overwhelmed with individual clients whom the staff were unwilling to turn away in the absence of any viable alternative service. At the same time many of the staff, and some of the Management Committee, felt that to concentrate exclusively on casework was to perform only a very limited function and they sought ways of extending the role of the Centre. This proved yet another source of debate, some of the Management Committee fearing what they interpreted as 'political' activity on the part of the Centre. Thus any extension of community-oriented work in such areas as housing, immigration, community relations or the enforcement of rights, was interpreted as a potential area of conflict with government, and as such, a threat to the 'non-political' role which it was felt proper for a lawyer to maintain in his professional capacity. These fears were very much to the fore amongst certain members of the local Law Society, and caused some friction between staff and representatives of that Society on the Management Committee who were anxious about the 'correct' role of the Centre.

A further matter of concern to the local Law Society was the belief that the Centre was undertaking too much legal aid work, particularly criminal work. It was claimed that private practitioners were losing legally aided clients to a Centre which operated at an advantage by virtue of the publicity it received. Had the Centre not been so financially dependent upon legal aid moneys, the staff would have been only too happy to reduce the amount of such work, since it would have enabled them to offer an entirely free legal service, as had been originally intended. However, in appealing to grant-giving bodies for funds, it was often stipulated that such financial help as could be made available should be used to supplement legal aid money, not to replace it; their emphasis lay in innovation and development, ironically often in those very areas of work which were viewed by some members of the legal profession as too 'political'.

It would, however, be a mistake to deduce from the foregoing that relationships with the profession were in general unsatisfactory. On the contrary, apart from a problem arising over the issue of waivers, relationships with the Law Society remained amicable throughout, and at the local level the criticisms appear to have emanated from a relatively small number of solicitors.

Relationships with the local authority were, however, less than satisfactory. About a year after the Centre opened it turned down an invitation to form part of a proposed Aid and Information Centre, feeling that by so doing it would lose its individuality, and furthermore that by sharing certain facilities with other organizations under the umbrella of the local authority, it would be seen by the community as an extension of local government. This refusal may have coloured the Council's view of the Centre which it believed was associated with pressure group activities in the north of the Borough and which were known to be hostile to the Council. Although the Centre denied this, the issue came to a head when, faced with probable closure due to lack of funds, the Centre approached the Council for help and was told that financial assistance in the form of a loan would only be made available providing the senior solicitor and two members of the Management Committee withdrew from their association with the Centre. Such a condition was totally unacceptable, and no funds were forthcoming from that source.

The somewhat tenuous relationship with the local authority, and one which pre-dated their refusal to co-operate with the Aid and Information Centre, may have had other, wider, financial repercussions. On two occasions the Centre submitted grant applications to the Home Office under the terms of the Urban Aid Programme, but on both occasions was turned down. The significance of this point lies in the fact that all such applications have to be submitted through the local authority who must not only agree to assume part of the financial responsibility for any programme funded in this way, but who are also responsible for allocating priorities to the various submissions.

The opinions of representatives of other local groups and agencies regarding the work of the Centre were generally quite positive, in so far as they agreed that the Centre made a very valuable contribution to the life of the area, and that its disappearance due to lack of funds would be a great loss. At a more fundamental level, the views of such agencies reflected their own interpretation of the essential ingredients of community work and the specific needs of the area. Whilst the older, more traditional agencies feared any extension of activity that might be regarded as radical, the more 'revolutionary' groups looked to the staff of the Centre for leadership and support through the use of their legal skills. Thus they expected the Centre to take a more active role in stimulating community organization; in the development of legal competence, and in demystifying the law for their clients. They were critical of the conventional role played by the staff as mediators, believing that this both supported the status quo and protected their own professionalism.

The effectiveness of the casework role of the Centre is difficult to assess. No attempt was made to evaluate the quality of the legal service offered, partly because there is no really adequate way of measuring this, and partly because the professional ethics of the legal profession prevented access to much relevant information. However, in interviews with clients, an attempt was made to assess the degree of their satisfaction, and the relevance of the help given. The vast majority were very satisfied with the way their case had been handled, indeed the extent of their gratitude was sometimes felt by the lawyers to be acutely embarrassing; they suggested that the type of client who used the Centre was not always sufficiently discerning about standards of service.

In the few cases where dissatisfaction was expressed the main sources of complaint were lack of adequate communication with the lawyer, inefficient administration, or the fact that an unfamiliar person appeared to represent them in court or at the tribunal hearing. Most clients said they would return to the Centre if they needed help on some future occasion, its informality being a particular feature which made it more approachable than other agencies.

At the same time it must be recognized that amidst the conflicting views concerning the goals of the Centre, there was one about which there was complete agreement, namely that it should provide a free legal service to all those living and working in the community. Yet despite the fact that the Centre dealt with an average of 1,500 cases a year, and that its resources in terms of finance and manpower were usually over-stretched, certain parts of its catchment area remained virtually untouched. Furthermore, in a sample of non-users whose addresses were selected on the basis of their proximity to users, over half were found to have no knowledge of the Centre at all. To the extent that these people appeared to suffer from many of the same problems as did those who used the Centre, and not to differ from them in terms of their demographic or social characteristics, it would seem that substantial areas of unmet legal need remain even within this relatively small catchment area.

It may be that the failure of a large section of the community to make use of the Law Centre reflects the widely held view expressed by those interviewed, that law, and not merely lawyers, is for 'them' not for 'us', and even the recognition that a problem is a legal one would not, under present circumstances, necessarily lead to the seeking of a legal solution.

In the final chapter we have briefly explored possible directions for the future development of law centres in the light of experience not only at North Kensington, but of the centres which later opened in and around London.

Chapter 8

EPILOGUE

In the Preface to this volume the setting up of a new type of centre - the Newham Rights Centre - was mentioned, and it was pointed out that delays encountered in setting up the Centre prevented any comparative study being undertaken. (1) Since then, however, a report on the Newham Rights Centre has been submitted to the Nuffield Foundation (2) and a very brief account of the principles and practices adopted there seems pertinent here, since they are very different from the more traditional approach described in this volume.

Without wishing to oversimplify the situation, the North Kensington Neighbourhood Law Centre and the Newham Rights Centre may be viewed as standing on opposite ends of a continuum representing the more traditional individualized approach to legal problems and the broader, community approach respectively. (3) In attempting this latter approach to what are in essence socio-legal problems, it was hoped to provide an opportunity for lawyers, social workers and community workers to share their knowledge and experience, and to involve the local community at grass roots level, not through any advisory board or committee, but through active involvement.

In practical terms it was felt that this multi-disciplinary aim could most appropriately be achieved by working with and through local groups, rather than dealing with individual cases. (4) The rationale underlying such an approach arose out of earlier work carried out by the present authors (5) in which four factors were highlighted: the socio-legal nature of most problems, particularly those experienced by financially and educationally disadvantaged people; the fragmentation of existing social services; the reluctance of many people to approach 'outsiders'; and the tendency of most professionals to deal with problems from only one perspective. Thus the internal organization of the Centre focused on the sharing of tasks, and job activity was determined in terms of time availability and accumulated knowledge, with the aim of minimizing the 'specialist' skills of professionals.

A great deal of initial public relations work had to be undertaken in order to establish local contacts and to make people aware of the Centre's existence and its intended function. As they were appointed, staff spent a considerable amount of time visiting local authority departments, talking to officials, to local lawyers, to voluntary agencies and to local groups such as tenants' associations. During this period of learning and making people aware of the Centre, it was often difficult to put across the policy of adopting a group emphasis and the staff were under pressure to be seen to be doing something in order to acquire credibility in the eyes of local residents. Initially the staff were not too dismayed since it gave them personally the opportunity to increase their skills and to accumulate knowledge in areas of law and general welfare rights concerning which they would later be helping groups to help themselves. Only gradually did the work expand in the ways initially intended, and individual cases made up a significant proportion of the Centre's work for the first year. (6)

A few examples of the kinds of work undertaken at the Newham Rights Centre may help to clarify the type of projects with which a community oriented Law Centre might become involved. (7) Working with local groups mostly entailed helping and advising tenants' associations and a few local pressure groups; often an embryo group had been formed but had not developed any further due to lack of resources or information. A few group cases were undertaken where the members of the group had a common cause or grievance, for example, against the same landlord. The educative role of the Centre concentrated on developing a comprehensive citizens' rights course, intended for representatives of local groups; on giving talks on specific topics at the invitation of local organizations; and on contributing to courses at the local polytechnic. Work with younger members of the community included co-ordinating play schemes in the area and assisting the local authority in running an intermediate treatment summer camp. The passing of the Health and Safety at Work Act, 1974, afforded members of the Centre the opportunity to interpret new legislation and assess its likely significance for unions and trades councils in the area. Further research on policy and legislation was undertaken on, for example, mental health legislation, social security benefits, and gas and electricity board policies. Last, but by no means least, the Centre acted as a very important resource and information centre, not only for local people but also for other professionals and workers in the area.

This brief account of some aspects of the projects undertaken by the Newham Rights Centre in no way does justice to the range and scope of its work. However, these examples are intended to provide some insight into an alternative approach to legal problems, in this case within a socio-legal framework aimed at the community as a whole rather than dealing with individual cases. The current work in law centres is an admixture of the casework and community approaches, the actual content varying according to the area served, the aims and objectives of the staff running them, and the constraints, such as finance, within which they are obliged to operate.

Leaving aside the variations in law centres concerning their work on a day-to-day basis, we should conclude by considering their future and the future of legal services in this country. A recent report of the Lord Chancellor's Office (8) has confirmed that the situation regarding legal services has changed very little in the years which have marked the dawning of the law centre era. It found that many people's legal rights are still going wholly by default, particularly those in the lower socio-economic groups, and, a severe overall shortage of solicitors exists, together with inadequate geographical coverage. Furthermore, much of the law affecting the most pressing problems of the poor, for example in the areas of housing and welfare rights, still remains outside expert assistance. Just as post-Beveridge the hoped-for 'cure' of the welfare state proved insufficient to treat the ills of the time, so efforts in the law centre field (which have not had the advantage of funding on a national scale and have necessarily been very local in emphasis) have not yet made any significant impact on the provision of legal services throughout the country.

Although the cataloguing of persistent deficiencies in the report of the Lord Chancellor is rather disheartening, three other recent developments throw a more positive light on the situation. First, a Royal Commission has been set up and this should be at work by the autumn. Second, the Lord Chancellor has announced that by saving legal aid money in undefended divorce cases more funds will be available to finance new law centres, and the legal aid limits will be raised, although we may be approaching 1980 before this becomes a reality. Third, the law centre movement has become organized into an official Law Centres Working Group, (9) comprising fourteen member centres. This group is committed to ensuring that existing law centres continue to thrive and to promoting the development of new ones; it also has the important function of disseminating information between centres and consolidating their position. The emergence of this group as an official body seems to signify that, six years after the opening of the first law centre, these agencies, in some shape or form, have established themselves as part of the fabric of legal services in this country.

APPENDIX A

THE RESEARCH

Obtaining access to the North Kensington Law Centre did not take place in ideal circumstances. Prior to the setting up of the Research Unit the Centre had on several occasions approached the Nuffield Foundation for funds, but had been unsuccessful. Since the Unit was initially established with a view to its monitoring and evaluating a number of different legal services programmes, it was clear from the outset that it would wish to include the North Kensington Centre - a pioneer in the field. After prolonged negotiations between the Centre and the Foundation, funds were made available on the condition that the Unit be allowed access for research purposes, and a researcher was appointed to the task for a period of one year, assisted by interviewers and coders as necessary.

METHOD

The method used was that of participant observation and it is perhaps useful to look at Cicourel's (1) continuum for the classification of the extent of participation:

1 Observer but non-participant
2 Observer as participant
3 Participant as observer
4 Fully fledged participant observer.

As far as any of these classifications applies to the research work at the Centre it is probably the 'observer as participant' which is the most appropriate. Since manpower is an essential element of the Centre and any 'observers' are quickly swept into the mainstream of helpers, this was inevitable. However it was fully understood before the researcher joined the Centre that she had a definite role of her own and this she tried to emphasize during the first few weeks. Once her presence as a researcher had been established it was easier to participate; her most common task was manning the reception desk although she occasionally undertook urgent errands when no other volunteer was available.

The research worker attended all meetings connected with the Centre as an observer, with no right to vote, and on such occasions was sometimes asked to provide information arising from the research findings, for example in connection with the organization of volunteers. Although it had previously been agreed that the staff and the research team should hold regular meetings, in practice these did not seem appropriate as the research was ongoing and the worker was always at the Centre and able to discuss with the staff informally.

ATTITUDES TO THE RESEARCH

The initial reaction of the staff was one of wariness and they acted with extreme caution. Very soon, however, the research worker was accepted as one of the team, it was recognized that she had her own particular job to do, and she received the fullest possible help and co-operation.

Perhaps the most difficult problem to overcome related to confidentiality; no access to the clients' files was allowed, and consent forms had to be used to obtain their agreement to be interviewed by the research team (see details Appendix C). Even the use of this form presented problems for the staff who feared that it introduced an element of obligation; clients would feel obliged to sign the form because the Centre was helping them. An attempt was made to overcome this by stressing to clients that the research was independent of the Centre, and that whether they signed the form or not would make no difference to the way their case was handled.

The research team proposed extending the amount of information to be completed on the record cards kept by the Centre in order to obtain a broader profile of clients. However, here too there were problems and the Centre staff strongly resisted the addition of categories relating to the clients' personal characteristics, particularly any record of race, since this information was not felt to be essential to conducting a client's case and could be considered divisive. At this time the format of record cards for the newer centres was being discussed and most of them adopted a more extended record sheet, the information from which could be collated by computer; however North Kensington decided to retain its own, abbreviated, cards. After lengthy discussions with the researcher they agreed to add one major piece of information, namely the employment status of clients. It was originally proposed that the term 'occupation' be added to the card, but this was felt by the staff to involve unnecessary questioning of clients and a compromise was reached using pre-coded categories: Employed/Unemployed/OAP/Housewife/Student. In addition, the layout of the card was revised, age groupings were added, and space allowed for the recording of both names and addresses of landlords in housing cases, and the work address and telephone number of clients. Unfortunately, despite these prolonged negotiations, an analysis of the record cards by the research worker showed that the new or revised categories were insufficiently used to make the resulting information meaningful.

Before the research worker joined, the Centre had also suggested using specially designed pads on which telephone messages would be recorded; in this way it was hoped that the research team would obtain information about emergency calls and contacts with outside agencies. This arrangement was thought to have the added advantage that it would enable the staff themselves to make a more accurate assessment of time spent on telephone calls for billing purposes. However this experiment also failed, since staff were either too rushed to fill in the sheets (in retrospect probably too much information was requested) or else they simply forgot.

APPENDIX B

WORK HANDLED BY THE CENTRE

The information set out in the following Tables B1 - 5 gives a picture of the type of work undertaken by the Centre during 1973.

TABLE B.1 Types of enquiry recorded at reception during 1973

Type of enquiry	January		February		March		April		May		June		July	
	No.	%	No.	%	No.	%	No.	%	No.	%	No.	%	No.	%
Housing	79	45.1	47	38.5	50	37.9	36	42.4	33	47.1	27	41.5	23	35.4
Crime (including juvenile)	17	9.7	21	17.2	22	16.7	12	14.1	13	18.6	19	29.2	17	26.2
All accidents	4	2.3	3	2.5	8	6.1	3	3.5	2	2.9	2	3.1	4	6.2
Consumer	6	3.4	11	9.0	4	3.0	0	0	5	7.1	5	7.7	1	1.5
Family	3	1.7	5	4.1	1	0.8	7	8.2	3	4.3	2	3.1	3	4.6
Matrimonial	15	8.6	12	9.8	12	9.1	5	5.9	7	10.0	3	4.6	7	10.8
Employment	11	6.3	1	0.8	13	9.9	3	3.5	1	1.4	1	1.5	2	3.1
Social security	3	1.7	2	1.6	1	0.8	1	1.2	1	1.4	1	1.5	0	0
Conveyancing	1	0.6	0	0	1	0.8	2	2.4	0	0	0	0	0	0
Miscellaneous**	35	20.0	19	15.6	19	14.4	9	10.6	4	5.7	4	6.2	7	10.8
No information	1	0.6	1	0.8	1	0.8	7	8.2	1	1.4	1	1.5	1	1.5
Total	175	100	122	100	132	100	85	100	70*	100	65	100	65	100

Type of enquiry	August		September		October		November		December		Total for year	
	No.	%	No.	%	No.	%	No.	%	No.	%	No.	%
Housing	11	35.4	26	41.3	21	31.4	36	27.1	7	23.3	396	37.6
Crime (including juvenile)	9	20.0	11	17.5	16	23.9	29	21.8	5	16.7	191	18.2
All accidents	0	0	3	4.8	1	1.5	7	5.3	1	3.3	38	3.6
Consumer	2	4.4	2	3.2	3	4.5	8	6.0	0	0	47	4.5
Family	4	8.9	3	4.8	6	9.0	5	3.8	1	3.3	43	4.1
Matrimonial	7	15.6	6	9.5	5	7.5	15	11.3	2	6.7	96	9.1
Employment	3	6.7	2	3.2	2	3.0	5	3.8	2	6.7	46	4.4
Social security	1	2.2	1	1.6	2	3.0	4	3.0	1	3.3	18	1.7
Conveyancing	0	0	0	0	0	0	5	3.8	1	3.3	10	1.0
Miscellaneous**	6	13.3	4	6.4	6	9.0	15	11.3	8	26.7	136	12.9
No information	2	4.4	5	8.0	5	7.5	4	3.0	2	6.7	31	3.0
Total	45	100	63	100	67	100	133	100	30	100	1052	100

* Includes one person with two types of enquiry.

** Miscellaneous includes e.g. help in filling in forms, queries over tax/gas bills, etc., how to get a commissioner for oaths, wanting to make a will, having letters explained, lost pawn tickets, enquiries about naturalization, wanting to change name, how to get a local plumber.

Source: Reception records

TABLE B.2 Addresses of callers to Law Centre reception (shown as percentages)

Address of caller	Jan.	Feb.	March	April	May	June	July	Aug.	Sept.	Oct.	Nov.	Dec.
Inside Catchment Area	53.8	57.4	58.3	65.3	73.9	73.9	61.5	62.8	68.2	51.6	66.8	70.0
Outside Catchment Area	29.1	31.2	22.1	20.4	20.3	26.1	39.3	30.2	27.0	37.8	27.0	20.0
No information	17.1	11.5	19.6	14.3	5.8	-	9.2	7.0	4.8	4.6	6.2	10.0
Total	100	100	100	100	100	100	100	100	100	100	100	100
N*	175	122	132	85	70	65	65	45	63	67	133	30

* N is the total sample number

Source: Reception records

TABLE B.3 Source of referral to Centre (1973)

Source		%
Local/informal contacts e.g. friend, saw it when passing etc.		54.7
Other agencies (statutory and voluntary)		27.4
Other solicitors		2.1
Courts/police		4.0
Other, e.g. doctor, media, post office		11.8
Total		100
	N	569

Source: Reception records

TABLE B.4 Referrals out made by the Centre (1973)

Outgoing referrals		%
Other law centres/advice centres		35.1
Private practice solicitors		53.4
Other agencies, e.g. housing action centre, CAB, claimants' union, rent officer		11.5
Total		100
	N	469

Source: Reception records

TABLE B.5 Monthly breakdown of types of cases handled at the Centre (1973)

Type of case	January		February		March		April		May		June		July	
	No.	%	No.	%	No.	%	No.	%	No.	%	No.	%	No.	%
Housing	58	40.3	40	46.0	45	31.5	42	38.9	54	37.0	54	41.2	35	38.4
Crime	41	28.5	18	20.7	41	28.7	30	27.8	51	34.9	44	33.6	28	30.8
Juvenile crime											4	3.1	3	3.3
All accidents	6	4.2	3	3.5	16	11.2	6	5.6	4	2.7	7	5.3	4	4.4
Consumer	8	5.6	7	8.1	9	6.3	4	3.7	4	2.7	5	3.8	1	1.1
Family	5	3.5	-	-	6	4.2	3	2.8	6	4.1	4	3.1	2	2.2
Employment	11	7.6	4	4.6	5	3.5	6	5.6	5	3.4	2	1.5	7	7.6
Miscellaneous	12	8.3	7	8.1	16	11.2	7	6.5	13	8.9	8	6.1	11	12.1
No information	3	2.1	8	9.2	5	3.5	10	9.3	9	6.2	3	2.3	-	-
Total	144	100	87	100	143	100	108	100	146	100	131	100	91	100

Type of case	August		September		October		November		December		Total for year	
	No.	%	No.	%	No.	%	No.	%	No.	%	No.	%
Housing	36	34.3	46	42.2	35	31.5	39	33.9	39	50.0	523	38.3
Crime	32	30.5	31	28.4	25	22.5	29	25.2	15	19.2	412	30.2
Juvenile crime	2	1.9	3	2.8	5	4.5	5	4.4	5	6.4		
All accidents	3	2.9	3	2.8	10	9.0	3	2.6	2	2.6	67	4.9
Consumer	11	10.5	7	6.4	11	9.9	7	6.1	7	9.0	81	5.9
Family	2	1.9	2	1.8	3	2.7	3	2.6	2	2.6	38	2.9
Employment	3	2.9	3	2.8	6	5.4	8	7.0	3	3.9	63	4.6
Miscellaneous	13	12.4	9	8.3	14	12.6	16	13.9	4	5.1	130	9.0
No information	3	2.9	5	4.6	2	1.8	5	4.4	1	1.3	54	4.0
Total	105	100	109	100	111	100	115	100	78	100	1368	100

Source: Law Centre record cards (figures collated from research and development officer's reports).

APPENDIX C

INTERVIEWS WITH CLIENTS

Access to clients was a pre-condition of the study, but one which met with very considerable resistance on the part of the legal profession over the issue of confidentiality. The researcher was not permitted to see files, nor to have access to record cards giving the names and addresses of clients. In view of the importance which was attached to obtaining clients' views, much time was devoted to negotiating with the staff of the Centre in order to find some method which would prove satisfactory to all concerned. At one point the Centre suggested contacting clients by letter, writing on behalf of the research worker to ask for an interview. This was rejected for a number of reasons: it would have been extremely time consuming (once the client had replied the research worker would then have had to make a further approach in order to arrange a convenient time), but more importantly it was felt that Law Centre clients would not be receptive to this type of approach, being generally unused to receiving formal communications through the post and equally unused to writing letters or making telephone calls themselves. The researcher then proposed that a 'consent form' be used at the reception desk which clients would be asked to sign if they were willing to be interviewed by a research worker at some future date. This was considered to be inappropriate by the Centre staff who thought that clients might feel they were being 'blackmailed' into signing if they wanted to receive help from the Centre. They did, however, agree to such a consent form being used at the time of the client's first interview with a volunteer lawyer.

The research worker spent a considerable amount of time briefing volunteers on the use of the forms, explaining that these were to be used at the end of the interview in order to avoid creating any barrier between lawyer and client. It was to be made clear to clients that they were under no obligation to sign, and that whether or not they did so would in no way affect their future dealings with the Centre.

Most volunteers were receptive to the idea, though some seemed to find it embarrassing to ask clients to sign - some simply forgot. As a result the research worker needed to be on hand a good deal of the time in order to give encouragement and reminders. It was hoped that a pool of names and addresses from which a sample could be drawn would be available within a few months. Unfortunately, due partly to fluctuations in the number of new clients attending the Centre and partly to the varying degrees of enthusiasm exhibited by the volunteers, it proved necessary to prolong the process and forms were being used for most of the research year.

Volunteers were also requested to make a note of any refusals, and in particular to record the clients' reasons for refusing. Unfortunately this information was only provided spasmodically (possibly because volunteers felt that a refusal might be seen by the researcher as a reflection on their ability to administer the form) and no reliable figures were forthcoming. Clearly this prevents any discussion of the extent and direction of possible bias.

A sample of 150 cases was drawn from the completed forms (roughly 10 per cent of the annual caseload) stratified by type of problem (see Table 4.1, p.33).

Once the name and address of a client had been ascertained, the staff of the Centre were asked to inform the research worker when the case was nearing completion. Uncompleted cases, involving long drawn-out negotiations, were left until the last few weeks of the research period thus allowing for a reasonable amount of contact between the client and the Centre.

In order to obtain a sample of 150 persons, a total of 201 contacts had to be attempted. Table C.1 shows the reasons for the 51 non-contacts and the types of problem for which they had consulted the Centre.

TABLE C.1 Non-contacts in client sample

Reason for non-contact	Type of problem					
	Housing	Crime	Employment	Family	Miscellaneous	Total
Moved away (no forwarding address available)	25	11	1	1	-	38
Not known at address given	2	3	-	-	-	5
Refused*	2	3	-	-	1	6
Respondent did not speak sufficient English	-	-	1	-	-	1
Respondent in custody	-	1	-	-	-	1
Total	29	18	2	1	1	51

* Despite the fact that they had signed a consent form.

By far the greatest number of non-contacts were people who had moved, a situation to be expected in an area where so many are displaced through housing problems. However, a substantial number of those who had consulted the Centre about a criminal matter had also moved and it can be speculated that they may have deemed it wiser to leave the area. There were very few outright refusals, although occasionally extra reassurance was needed from the interviewer concerning confidentiality.

The bulk of the interviewing was done by two part-time interviewers over a period of eight months. The interview schedule used mainly open-ended questions and was designed with a view to exploring clients' difficulties and their experiences at the Centre; several questions focusing on general attitudes to the law and the legal system were also included. Interviews lasted between 1½ and 2 hours, but the interviewers frequently spent extended periods of time, sometimes a whole evening, with clients who needed supportive help, or who felt the need to talk over their problems.

Demographic details concerning the sample of clients are set out in Tables C.2 and C.3.

TABLE C.2 Sample of clients showing age, marital status and birthplace

	MEN		WOMEN	
	No.	%	No.	%
AGE				
0 - 16	1	1.1	1	1.8
17 - 25	24	25.3	11	20.0
26 - 40	33	34.7	20	36.4
41 - 59	22	23.2	19	34.5
60 and over	15	15.8	4	37.3
Total	95	100	55	100
MARITAL STATUS				
Single	36	37.9	14	25.5
Married/Cohabitee	47	49.5	23	41.8
Divorced/separated	10	10.5	13	23.6
Widowed	2	2.1	5	9.1
Total	95	100	55	100
BIRTHPLACE				
North Kensington	13	13.7	8	14.5
Kensington and Chelsea	0	-	0	-
Elsewhere in London	19	20.0	13	23.6
Elsewhere in England/Wales/Scotland	22	23.2	10	18.2
Ireland (North & South)	18	19.0	10	18.2
West Indies	12	12.6	6	10.9
India or Pakistan	1	1.1	0	-
Elsewhere*	10	10.5	8	14.5
Total	95	100	55	100

* Includes Germany, Spain, Canada, Australia, South Africa, Nigeria, Sierra Leone, St Helena, Ghana, Zanzibar, Hungary, Guyana.

TABLE C.3 Sample of clients' socio-economic groupings of households

Socio-economic group	No.	%	
Registrar General Category I - professional, managerial	1	0.7	
Registrar General Category II - intermediate	1	0.7	
Registrar General Category III NM - skilled non-manual	30	20.0	
Registrar General Category III M - skilled manual	39	26.0	76.0
Registrar General Category IV - semi-skilled	45	30.0	
Registrar General Category V - unskilled	24	16.0	
Unemployed	3	2.0	
Student	6	4.0	
No information	1	0.7	
Total	150	100	

INERVIEWS WITH NON-USERS

METHOD

Interviews were conducted with 100 local residents who had not used the Centre. A random sample of 100 addresses of actual clients was taken and interviewers were asked to call at the nearest house or flat, alternating between approaching houses to the right or left of the address and alternating between floors, where the houses were divided into flats, e.g. taking the top flat at the first house, the basement flat at the next, the middle flat at the next and so on. In this way it was hoped to achieve a reasonably unbiased sample, as well as to avoid selecting pockets of the borough where information about the Centre was limited.

Interviews took place during a three week period in the summer and were conducted by two experienced interviewers. They lasted for between half and three quarters of an hour and involved the use of both open-ended and closed questions. The schedule was designed to find out the extent of non-users' knowledge of the Centre and whether or not they had faced similar problems to those taken by clients to the Centre. Non-users were presented with a list of potential problems, and if they had experienced them, what action they had taken and with what success. Others were asked how they might handle such problems if they arose in the future. The examples chosen were those with a potential legal solution and/or of the type taken by clients to the Law Centre. Other areas of questioning concerned their knowledge of legal aid and their use of, and attitudes towards, solicitors; these latter questions were similar to those asked of the clients. Tables D.1 and D.2 give demographic information regarding the sample.

TABLE D.1 Sample of non-users showing age, marital status and birthplace

	Men		Women	
	No.	%	No.	%
AGE				
0 - 16	0	-	0	-
17 - 25	5	11.4	11	19.6
26 - 40	15	34.1	17	30.4
41 - 59	9	20.5	10	17.9
60 and over	15	34.1	18	32.1
Total	44	100	56	100
MARITAL STATUS				
Single	12	27.3	9	16.1
Married/Cohabitee	24	54.5	30	53.6
Divorced/separated	3	6.8	4	7.1
Widowed	5	11.4	13	23.2
Total	44	100	56	100
BIRTHPLACE				
North Kensington	7	15.9	7	12.5
Remainder of Kensington and Chelsea	5	11.4	3	5.4
Elsewhere in London	10	22.7	14	25.0
Elsewhere in England/Wales/Scotland	7	15.9	8	14.3
Ireland (North & South)	2	4.5	8	14.3
West Indies	3	6.8	6	10.7
India or Pakistan	0	-	0	-
Elsewhere*	10	22.7	10	17.9
Total	44	100	56	100

* Includes Spain, Portugal, Gibraltar, Russia, South Africa, Nigeria, Morocco, Hungary, New Zealand, Australia, Asia Minor, Montserrat, Poland, Malta and Greece

TABLE D.2 Sample of non-users' socio-economic groupings of households

Socio-economic group	%*	
Registrar General Category I - professional/managerial	3	
Registrar General Category II - intermediate	7	
Registrar General Category III NM - skilled non-manual	12	} 64
Registrar General Category III M - skilled manual	28	}
Registrar General Category IV - semi-skilled	24	}
Registrar General Category V - unskilled	17	
Unemployed	1	
Student	1	
No information	7	
Total	100	

* NB: Percentages coincide with numbers since total number of respondents = 100.

NOTES

CHAPTER 1 GENERAL BACKGROUND

1 Almost all these have been set up in the London area where, in August 1974 there were eleven such centres, and one in Cardiff.
2 For details, see B. Abel-Smith and R. Stevens: 'Lawyers and the Courts', Heinemann Educational Books (1967).
3 See the 'Report of the Committee on Legal Aid and Advice in England and Wales' (1945).
4 Mainly Poor Man's Lawyer sessions attached to settlements in major cities. Voluntary legal advisers also operated through Citizens Advice Bureaux, clubs, organisations and trade unions.
5 See the 1945 Report, para. 125.
6 The Legal Aid Committee is subject only to the general guidance of the Lord Chancellor who in turn is responsible to Parliament for the implementation of the Act.
7 Legal Aid and Advice Act 1949, amended in 1960 to raise income limits and again in 1964 to allow for the recovery of costs against the Legal Aid Fund.
8 The original advice scheme, which was provided for by the 1949 Act, was to have consisted of 98 salaried solicitors operating in 250 centres throughout the country - on this see Seton Pollock: Legal Aid as a Social Service, 'Law Society's Gazette', 399, June 1970.
9 Memorandum on Legal Aid and Advice prepared by the Council of the Law Society at the request of the Lord Chancellor's Advisory Committee.
10 Some of the ideas put forward by the Law Society at that time were incorporated into the Legal Advice and Assistance Act 1972.
11 'Lord Chancellor's Office Report on Legal Aid and Advice in England and Wales 1969-1970' (July 1971).
12 Ibid., para. 7.

CHAPTER 2 SETTING UP THE NORTH KENSINGTON NEIGHBOURHOOD LAW CENTRE

1 C. Dickens: 'Household Words' (1850).
2 C. Booth: 'Life and Labour of the People in London' (1903)

3 M. Adeney: 'Community Action: Four Examples', Runnymede Trust Publication (May 1971).

4 1971 Census: quoted in 'London Facts and Figures', GLC (1972).

5 1971 Census, the 1966 census quoted in 'The Notting Hill Summer Project Interim Report', Notting Hill Housing Service (1969), showed that over half the children aged up to 15 lived in North Kensington.

6 A statistic cited in R. Milton and E. Morrison: 'A Community Project in Notting Dale', Allen Lane, The Penguin Press (1972).

7 'Tomorrow's London', A background to the Greater London Development Plan (GLC 1969).

8 Strictly speaking Notting Hill is the south-east corner of North Kensington, but quite frequently, as in the examples given, is taken to mean a larger area, being almost synonymous with North Kensington.

9 From J. Wilkenden: 'Colour in Britain', Oxford University Press for the Institute of Race Relations (1958) quoted in Milton and Morrison, op.cit.

10 Although the 1971 census figures have subsequently become available, to update the table would have been a major task and unlikely to have changed the overall picture painted here.

11 For a discussion of these problems see: A. Shonfield and S. Shaw (eds): 'Social Indicators and Social Policy', SSRC (1972).

12 Subsequent research findings suggest that many of these problems exist primarily at the top of the hierarchy. There is a considerable amount of co-operation at the lower levels.

13 North Kensington Neighbourhood Law Centre: Outline Proposals, 1969.

14 Ibid.

15 It is worth pointing out however that some of the newer centres receive substantial funds from their local authority.

16 Another charity contributed £5,000 for the second and third years, and £1,000 during the fourth; a further charity also made donations of £3,500 and £3,000 for the third and fourth years.

17 In practice, with a few individual donations the sum was made up to £5,840 and over £9,000 was recovered from legal aid moneys.

18 Memorandum of the Law Society, July 1969, quoted in the 'First Annual Report' of the North Kensington Neighbourhood Law Centre, February 1971.

19 In their Annual Report of 1969 the Charity Commissioners defined 'political' as 'any act designed to procure a change in the law'.

20 The first chairman, a QC, recalled that his tasks included electrical re-wiring, procuring and shifting second-hand furniture and acquiring second-hand office machines and a supply of law books.

21 For details of method see Appendices.

22 The literature is too extensive to cite in full but see for example, the 'Final Report of the OEO Legal Services Program, Evaluation Division', vol.1, prepared by John Kettelle Corporation, October 1971 and E. Baldwin: Evaluating the OEO Legal Services Program, 'Working Papers', July 1972.

23 See P. Morris, J. Cooper and A. Byles: Public Attitudes to Problem Definition and Problem Solving: A Pilot Study, 'British Journal of Social Work', vol.3, no.3, 1973.

24 Three of these were also members of the Management Committee and this involved a 'dual' interview.
25 See especially the 'Final Report of the OEO Legal Services Program'.
26 It is possible to give accurate advice but this does not necessarily ensure that a client is able to make use of it.

CHAPTER 3 THE DEVELOPMENT OF THE CENTRE

1 And it re-elects itself each year.
2 After the research period the Constitution was amended to allow for six representatives of the Advisory Council.
3 A member of staff had attributed this to the fact that, particularly in the early days, the pressure of work left them too weary to give their attention to such issues.
4 This view was emphasised in view of the pioneering role of the Centre. It was feared that any unpleasant publicity would damage the chances of support for future law centres.
5 It was originally planned that non-staff committee members should attend the Centre during evening sessions, on a rota basis, but such an arrangement was never followed.
6 These will be referred to in more detail in chapter 5 and are outlined in the Centre's 'Fourth Annual Report' (May 1974).
7 It was estimated that 200 people called at the Centre for advice during its first three weeks of operation: 'Guardian' report, 1 February 1971.
8 Figures produced by the research and development officer showed that over £4,000 a year was being spent in Counsel's fees which would amply cover the salary of a full-time solicitor-advocate (the 1974 annual report shows £5,883 spent in Counsel's fees).
9 Fears of 'political' involvement, see p.15f.
10 In addition he was very active in publicizing the activities of the Centre and in encouraging others to establish law centres in other parts of the country.
11 Such an approach involves a programme designed to achieve social change by means of a transfer of economic and political power to the poor community and the active involvement of the staff in such a programme.
12 It should again be noted that at an informal level such relationships were very friendly and this in itself may have contributed to an unwillingness to 'rock the boat' by pressing for goals to be clearly defined.
13 Several expressed a wish to work in a neighbourhood law centre when fully qualified and by the end of the research period two had become solicitors at other law centres.
14 Since the research was completed, 'kits' are now provided for this purpose to all volunteers.
15 For further material on people's views about solicitors see P. Morris, J. Cooper and A. Byles: Public Attitudes to Problem Definition and Problem Solving: A Pilot Study, 'British Journal of Social Work', vol.3, no.3.
16 This move was no doubt encouraged by the expansion of community (i.e. non-legal) work undertaken by new law centres being set up in other boroughs.

17 It should nevertheless be borne in mind that this occurred at a time of grave financial crisis, and was of a temporary nature.

18 As mentioned earlier the council has made premises available at a peppercorn rent.

19 As only approximately £10,000 has been received in donations each year the Centre has had to content itself with the latter sum, approximately £20,000 being derived annually from legal aid moneys.

20 For an interesting discussion of council control of independent groups, particularly as it affects Community Development Projects see J. Edginton: The Batley Battle, 'New Society', 5 September 1974.

21 Receipts from legal aid work, both criminal and civil, amounted to approximately £23,000 in 1973 ('Fourth Annual Report', May 1974).

22 In its Annual Report for 1974 the Centre reaffirmed its preference for funding by means of a national grant, to be independently administered (i.e. not through the Law Society).

23 Considerable confusion surrounds this issue: in an article in the 'Law Society's Gazette' (North Kensington Law Centre, 11 September 1974) Charles Wegg-Prosser wrote:

> It is wrongly thought by some people, possibly as a result of some injudicious 'off the cuff' remarks made recently by the Chairman of the British Legal Association, that solicitors in private practice are opposed to law centres. All the evidence is that this is not so, and that the legal profession and its responsible elected representatives have long seen that there is a role for salaried solicitors in fields which had formerly been thought of as the preserve of the private practitioner.

Recurring comments at Management Committee meetings led the present authors to believe that at grass roots there remains a considerable suspicion and resentment, although the 'official' view may well be as Mr Wegg-Prosser described it.

24 These are cases not yet completed but for which the eventual claim for legal aid moneys can be estimated.

25 The Urban Aid Programme was launched in January 1969; under it, some £60-65 million was to be channelled into areas of special need by 1976 'to relieve needs resulting from overcrowding, inadequate housing and schools, and from other symptoms of multiple deprivation' (Home Office press notice, 21 January 1969).

26 In July 1974, the Lord Chancellor announced that a sum of £50,000 would be provided to assist independent law centres and since then North Kensington has received support from that source, which was increased to £100,000 in 1975.

27 Since the research period one of the solicitors now supervises the book-keeping and accounts.

28 It was a matter of amazement to at least one committee member that staff should have to be told to hold meetings. He regarded this as a vital factor in good internal organization and one which should have been well known to all concerned.

29 This Centre eventually opened in March 1974.

30 The Centre later apologized for this to the Council.

31 'Evening Standard' 9 May 1973 banner headline, The Siege of Notting Hill.

32 Velvet-glove police treatment 'commendable', Paul Dobson, 'Kensington News and Post', 1 June 1973.
33 This coincided with local authority funding of law centres in a number of other boroughs. In Kensington and Chelsea the council had confined its help to providing premises for the Centre at a low rent.
34 Legal Advice and Assistance Act 1972, Part II.
35 These waivers exempt solicitors from certain Practice Rules, particularly those preventing them from advertising, sharing costs with anyone other than a solicitor, and charging less than the scale fees laid down by rules of court.
36 See note 23, this chapter.
37 On 30 July 1974, the Lord Chancellor announced in Parliament his intention of giving £50,000 to these neighbourhood law centres which might be threatened with closure at the end of the year due to lack of funds. A sum of £100,000 was similarly made available in 1975.

CHAPTER 4 THE CENTRE AT WORK

1 Since January 1973 the manning of this service has been shared with another law centre which has an adjoining catchment area.
2 The arrangement at the time of the research whereby each volunteer is responsible to one full-time solicitor developed over time and seemed to work quite well. Earlier attempts to have all volunteers supervised by one full-time staff member were less satisfactory.
3 See note 7, chapter 3.
4 At the time of the research each solicitor was handling up to 200 cases, at any one time.
5 See note 4, chapter 3.
6 In discussing proposals for monitoring with one of the new law centres, the representative of the Law Society on their Management Committee made quite clear that it was not the policy of law centres to undertake work of that nature.
7 Many, including the present writers, would question the implication that social work is a-political; however, later discussion with the solicitor concerned indicated a differing interpretation of the term 'political', his use of it being confined to the organization of group activity, with a view to achieving self-help.
8 Since then a Housing Unit has been set up, but at the time of writing this had not been in existence long enough to assess its impact.
9 Although these sheets were filled out by the receptionist whenever possible the total is an underestimate of the actual number of enquiries since at busy periods, or when a relief receptionist took over, entries were missed; the table should therefore be taken as a general guide rather than as a record of actual numbers. The average number of enquiries per month was probably nearer 150-200.
10 1971 Census.
11 It should be borne in mind that the information recorded at the reception desk included telephone enquiries as well as personal visits.

12 At times some concern was expressed by staff of other local agencies about this decision since it was recognized that landlords were sometimes in a worse position than their tenants.
13 Again, many solicitors in private practice undertake cases free of charge but keep no record of the numbers thus helped.
14 Before the Centre was set up this was the only firm offering a general service under the legal aid scheme. Subsequently the firm concentrated chiefly on matrimonial problems and, where relevant, referred other types of cases to the Centre.
15 For further references see chapter 5.
16 For details of the research method used in contacting clients see Appendix C.
17 For further details of the monthly distribution of cases handled by the Centre during 1973 see Table B.5, Appendix B.
18 A request was made for similar information to be recorded concerning the background of all clients calling at the Centre for comparative purposes. Unfortunately this was not carried out in a consistent manner and such data as were made available had to be discarded.
19 According to the record cards kept at the Centre clients were most frequently male; however, when a couple attended the Centre together, it was most likely that the husband's name would be recorded.
20 B. Glastonbury, M. Burdett and R. Austin: Community Perceptions of the Personal Social Services, 'Policy and Politics' vol.I, no.3, 1973, reported poor public knowledge of personal social services and a largely negative perception of those who used them. See also A. McKay, E.M. Goldberg and D. Fruin: Consumers and a Social Services Department, 'Social Work Today' vol.4, no.16, November 1973, who, in respect of a social service department, report that less than one third of consumers knew what to expect, and that there was a link between lack of expectations and lack of knowledge about the department.
21 For a discussion of the problems associated with the assessment of performances see D. Rosenthal, R. Kagan and D. Quatrone: 'Volunteer Attorneys and Legal Services for the Poor: New York's CLO Program', Russell Sage Foundation (1971).
22 Care should be taken when interpreting this table since the numbers are for the most part very small.
23 It seems likely that some who might have wished to criticize would be reluctant to do so in a research interview, fearing that it might make them appear ungrateful or disloyal.
24 During the year in question volunteer schoolchildren were used to redecorate the Centre throughout one weekend; not surprisingly the results were not up to professional standards.
25 Defined by the client as legal.
26 There was a fairly widespread belief that the Centre dealt only with various types of housing problem.
27 The fact that they had committed an offence did not necessarily mean that they considered themselves to be guilty. For a further discussion of this point see P. Morris, in P. Morris, R. White and P. Lewis, 'Social Needs and Legal Action', Martin Robertson (1972), p.67.
28 But added: 'I got two years instead of ten.'

29 Two people interviewed were unaware that the person they had seen was in fact a solicitor.
30 Morris, et al., op.cit., p.52.
31 It should be noted that most of the comments by clients concerning solicitors at the Centre related to the volunteer lawyers rather than the full-time legal staff who, on occasion, were known to spend considerable time discussing such problems.

CHAPTER 5 THE CENTRE AND THE COMMUNITY

1 See chapter 3.
2 This pattern is changing and the addition of new staff has resulted in an increasing number being recruited from outside. Furthermore redevelopment of the area has meant a reduction in available staff housing.
3 As the pioneer centre, North Kensington has from time to time been given considerable national publicity by the media, and the staff have made individual contributions to discussion and debate on radio and television.
4 For details of the non-user sample see Tables D.1 and D.2, Appendix D.
5 For details of research method see Appendix D. This aspect of the work was intended as a means of finding out the extent of non-users' knowledge of the Centre and whether or not they had experienced problems similar to those of 'users'. It was not intended as a representative sample of the residents of the area.
6 The staff at the Centre were aware that even within its catchment area there was a tendency for clients to cluster in certain nearby streets. However, further publicity was consciously avoided for fear of increasing the caseload unduly, and some concern was expressed about the research interviews with non-users in case this resulted in an upsurge of clients.
7 F. Raymond Marx in a study of 1,496 low-income people in three large American cities found that when presented with ten hypothetical problems, each of which had a potentially legal solution, to only one problem did as many as 52 per cent suggest consulting a lawyer. In six of the ten problems, less than 30 per cent suggested seeing a lawyer. 'The Legal Needs of the Poor: A Critical Analysis', American Bar Association, Chicago (1971).
8 In earlier work carried out by the unit it was noted that people might suggest sources of help for others which they themselves would not consider. See P. Morris, J. Cooper and A. Byles: Public Attitudes to Problem Definition and Problem Solving: A Pilot Study, 'British Journal of Social Work', vol.3, no.3.
9 Nine of these respondents made explicit reference to the Poor Man's Lawyer or Legal Aid.
10 It must be borne in mind that the original question related only to problems experienced during the preceding three years. Furthermore conveyancing, a matter with which the Law Centre did not deal, was omitted from the list.
11 In the following sections data obtained from both users and non-users is included.
12 See Gerald Sanctuary, Advertising the Legal Aid Scheme, 'Law Gazette', 12 September, 1973.

13 For further discussion and systematic analysis of attitudes to the legal system using scaling techniques see B. Abel-Smith et al.: 'Legal Problems and the Citizen', Heinemann (1973).
14 P. Morris et al., Public Attitudes to Problem Definition and Problem Solving: A Pilot Study, 'British Journal of Social Work', vol.3, no.3, 1973.
15 In using the word 'traditional' we mean that the law was seen as fair and desirable in so far as it was a satisfactory, indeed, essential, means of maintaining order in society.
16 Three of these were also members of the Centre's Management Committee.
17 One local solicitor expressed considerable surprise on hearing this, being unaware that 'the Centre got on so well with the police'.
18 During the course of our earlier work in the Borough the Select Committee on Race Relations visited North Kensington. See 'Select Committee on Race Relations Session 1971-72 Police/ Immigrant Relations Minutes of Evidence', 9 and 10 February, 1972, HMSO.
19 The solicitors claimed that very often clients were under the care of a social worker and/or other agency before they reached the Centre.
20 In this they echoed the views of the more senior legal members of the Management Committee.
21 It must, however, be borne in mind that for most clients this was in fact precisely the type of service they claimed to want.
22 Whereby an unrepresented defendant can be accompanied in court by a friend or adviser with whom he may confer, but the friend/ adviser may not address the court (McKenzie v McKenzie 1970 3WLR 472).
23 No figures are available since staff refused to allow us to record information of this nature which they saw as being divisive.
24 Two black clients, on separate occasions, had in anger forced their way through doors at the Centre (which were intended to be kept shut).
25 A Law Society Joint Committee on Law Centres was set up to discuss these and other problems, and the matter of waivers was finally resolved in consultation with the Lord Chancellor's Office.
26 Legal Action Group: 'Legal Services for the Future: Towards a New Framework for Legal Services', (May 1974). Law Centres' Working Group: 'Community Law Centres - Towards Equal Justice' (September 1974).

CHAPTER 6 WHERE NEXT?

1 S. Brakel: Free Services for the Poor: Staffed Offices vs Judicare, 'Wisconsin Law Review', vol.no.2, 1973, pp.532 ff.
2 'Justice for All', Society of Labour Lawyers, Fabian Research Series, 273 (1968) p.61.
3 An appendix to 'Justice for All' gives an account of the American programmes but in the text of the main report it is not suggested that law centres in this country should perform the same functions.

4 For a general discussion of this issue see P. Morris, R. White and P Lewis: 'Social Needs and Legal Action', Martin Robertson (1973).
5 Memorandum on Legal Aid and Advice prepared by the Council of the Law Society, February 1968, para. 24.
6 Clearly this is an over-simplification of the argument; all we wish to do here is draw attention to this multi-disciplinary approach.
7 See R. Kramer: 'Participation of the Poor', Prentice-Hall (1969) and D.H. Lowenstein and M.J. Waggoner: The New Wave in Legal Services for the Poor, 'Harvard Law Review', 805 (1967).
8 See J.E. Carlin: Storefront Lawyers in San Francisco, 'Transaction', vol.7, April 1970, pp.64-73. This may lead one to question whether the aim of transferring power to the poor community through self-help organizations is essentially a reflection of middle-class behaviour, where lawyers are used extensively to help mobilize power through group organization.
9 A.K. Pye points out that it is virtually inevitable that centres should be overwhelmed with individual cases since 'the demand for legal services increases directly in proportion to their availability and the publicity accorded to them'. See The Role of Legal Services in the Anti-Poverty Programme, 'Law and Contemporary Problems', vol.31, 1966.
10 From a review by R. Dworkin of Martin Meyer's book, 'The Lawyers'. Reprinted in R. Schwartz and J. Skolnick (eds): 'Society and the Legal Order', Basic Books, New York (1970).
11 It is recognized that this view is not shared by everyone; whilst David Donnison argues (Ideologies and Politics, 'Journal of Social Policy', April 1972) that ideologies must precede the search for goals, David Braybrooke and Charles Lindblom ('A Strategy of Decision', Free Press, New York, 1963) argue that a comprehensive ideology is not possible in view of the complexity of the problems presented, and the number of choices available. They refer to policy-making based upon 'disjointed incrementalism' adding decision to decision, and muddling through.
12 Referring to the vague and differing criteria upon which law centres currently operate, Susan Marsden-Smedley, director of the Legal Action Group, in Small Earthquake at LCO, 'New Law Journal', 8 August 1974, comments: 'A government of civil servants are understandably reluctant to hand over money to organizations that have no expressed operating criteria and might therefore in theory alter shape like a jellyfish in response to new perceived pressures or demands.'
13 See, for example, The Huge Cost of Going to Law, 'Sunday Times', 10 November 1974.
14 The 'social' aspects of middle-class legal problems are likely to be less obtrusive partly because the resources available allow them to adopt alternative solutions to these additional problems, and partly because the nature of their legal problems tends to differ in important ways from those of the poor.
15 This list is not intended to be comprehensive. The discussion falls outside the scope of this particular piece of research, but for a very full coverage see B. Christensen: 'Lawyers for People of Moderate Means', American Bar Association, Chicago (1970).

CHAPTER 8 EPILOGUE

1 It is, in fact, questionable whether such an approach would have been appropriate or desirable, bearing in mind the very different natures and aims of these two centres. Also the comparative method carries with it the inherent dangers of providing policy makers with material to support 'best buy' decisions, not usually intended in the research design.
2 This was an internal report and no material from this study has yet been published.
3 It should be stressed that since the research was concluded, the North Kensington Neighbourhood Law Centre has extended many aspects of its work to include the local community and local groups.
3 The experience of earlier centres, like North Kensington, confirmed the belief that once casework has been undertaken it is very difficult for staff to find the time to turn their attention to the broader aspects of community need, particularly if there is no alternative agency to which individuals can be referred.
5 See P. Morris, J. Cooper and A. Byles: Public Attitudes to Problem Definition and Problem Solving: A Pilot Study, 'British Journal of Social Work', vol.3, no.3.
6 This situation was not really remedied until the Centre had moved into its permanent premises, had instigated a free evening advice session, manned on a voluntary basis by local lawyers, social workers and accountants, and had accumulated sufficient knowledge of other local groups and agencies to build up a coherent referral network.
7 These examples are drawn from the research period July 1974 - December 1975; it must be remembered that since that time some aspects of the work will have expanded, others contracted, and new areas will have been explored.
8 Statement by the Lord Chancellor, 15 June 1976.
9 This group met informally over two years with the membership increasing as more centres opened; the North Kensington Neighbourhood Law Centre was one of the founder members.

APPENDIX A THE RESEARCH

1 A.V. Cicourel: 'Method and Measurement in Sociology', Free Press, New York (1964).

BIBLIOGRAPHY

ABEL-SMITH, B. and STEVENS, R., 'Lawyers and the Courts', Heinemann Educational Books, London, 1967.

ABEL-SMITH, B., ZANDER, M. and BROOKE, R., 'Legal Problems and the Citizen', Heinemann, 1973.

ADENEY, M., 'Community Action: Four Examples', Runnymede Trust Publication, May 1971.

BALDWIN, F., Evaluating the OEO Legal Services Program, 'Working Papers', July 1972.

BRAKEL, S., Free Services for the Poor: Staffed Offices vs Judicare, 'Wisconsin Law Review', vol.no.2, 1973.

BRAYBROOKE, D. and LINDBLOM, C., 'A Strategy of Decision', Free Press, New York, 1963.

CARLIN, J.E., Storefront Lawyers in San Francisco, 'Transaction', vol.7, April 1970.

CHRISTENSEN, B., 'Lawyers for People of Moderate Means', American Bar Association, Chicago, 1970.

CICOUREL, A.V., 'Method and Measurement in Sociology', Free Press, New York, 1964.

CONSERVATIVE POLITICAL CENTRE, 'Rough Justice', 1968.

DONNISON, D., Ideologies and Politics, 'Journal of Social Policy', April 1972.

EDGINGTON, J., The Batley Battle, 'New Society', 5 September 1974.

GLASTONBURY, B., BURDETT, M. and AUSTIN, R., Community Perceptions of the Personal Social Services, 'Policy and Politics', vol.1, no.3, 1973.

JOHN KETTELLE CORPORATION, 'Final Report of the OEO Legal Services Program, Evaluation Division', vol.1, October 1971.

KRAMER, R., 'Participation of the Poor', Prentice-Hall, Englewood Cliffs, NJ, 1969.

LAW CENTRES' WORKING GROUP, 'Community Law Centres - Towards Equal Justice', September 1974.

LEGAL ACTION GROUP, 'Legal Services for the Future: Towards a New Framework for Legal Services', May 1974.

'Lord Chancellor's Office Report on Legal Aid and Advice in England and Wales 1969-1970', July 1971.

LOWENSTEIN, D.H. and WAGGONER, M.J., The New Wave in Legal Services for the Poor, 'Harvard Law Review', 805, 1967.

MCKAY, A., GOLDBERG, E.M. and FRUIN, D., Consumers and a Social Services Department, 'Social Work Today', vol.4, no.16, November 1973.
MARX, F.R., 'The Legal Needs of the Poor: A Critical Analysis', American Bar Association, Chicago, 1971.
MILTON, R. and MORRISON, E., 'A Community Project in Notting Dale', Allen Lane, The Penguin Press, Harmondsworth, 1972.
MORRIS, P., COOPER, J. and BYLES, A., Public Attitudes to Problem Definition and Problem Solving: A Pilot Study, 'British Journal of Social Work', vol.3, no.3, 1973.
MORRIS, P., WHITE, R. and LEWIS, P., 'Social Needs and Legal Action', Martin Robertson, London, 1972.
POLLOCK, S., Legal Aid as a Social Service, 'Law Society's Gazette', 399, June 1970.
PYE, A.K., The Role of Legal Services in the Anti-Poverty Program, 'Law and Contemporary Problems', vol.31, 1966.
'Report of the Committee on Legal Aid and Advice in England and Wales' under the chairmanship of Lord Rushcliffe, HMSO, Cmnd.6641, London, 1945.
ROSENTHAL, D., KAGAN, R. and QUATRONE, D., 'Volunteer Attorneys and Legal Services for the Poor: New York's CLO Program', Russell Sage Foundation, 1971.
SCHWARTZ, R. and SKOLNICK, J. (eds), 'Society and the Legal Order', Basic Books, New York, 1970.
'Select Committee on Race Relations Session 1971-72, Police/Immigrant Relations Minutes of Evidence', 9 and 10 February 1972, HMSO.
SHONFIELD, A. and SHAW, S. (eds), 'Social Indicators and Social Policy', SSRC, 1972.
Society of Labour Lawyers, 'Justice for All', Fabian Research Series, 273, 1968.